AF575263

Rivers of Transformation

The Journey of Nine At-Risk Boys on a Twenty-Eight Day Canoe Trip

Jason Sullivan

Pine Grove
Press

The events and conversations in this book have been set down to the best of the author's ability. Names have been changed to protect privacy. Boys' journal entries and articles are used with permission. These entries have been unaltered, with the exception of spelling, to preserve the boys' character.

Photographs used with permission.
Maps © Mapbox, © OpenStreetMap

Cover Design: Allison Parrish
Cover Photo: Rodrigo De Mendoza on Unsplash

Library of Congress Control Number: 2019916178

ISBN: 978-1-7341409-0-3

Printed in the United States of America

Dedicated to:

Tyler
Logan
Zach
Caleb
Jaylen
Will
Robert
Mitchell
Chad
Chief Mike
Chief Travis

who accompanied me on this journey which
will remain ingrained in my heart;

the people we encountered on the river
who enriched our experience;

and all the other campers, past and present,
who make camp possible.

Contents

"All genuine learning is active, not passive. It involves the use of the mind, not just the memory. It is a process of discovery, in which the student is the main agent, not the teacher."

Mortimer Adler[1]

Introduction

Nestled in nine hundred acres of pine forest in North Carolina sprawls Cameron Boys Camp. The vivid blue sky of summer against the green and brown of the trees can soothe the soul of anyone willing to gaze into its beauty. Deer flash their tails nearby as a group of ten boys and three counselors ramble the trails to and fro. Green anole lizards scurry up the nearest scrub oak under the towering pines as the boys tromp past. Distinct calls of pileated woodpeckers cause newer boys' eyebrows to rise and ask their fellow campers if there are monkeys in these woods.

During morning walks from the campsite to the dining hall, the boys observe spider webs jeweled in dew. They've learned to walk slowly, taking in the majesty of the forest with their eyes, nose, ears, and skin. So much can be learned from observing one's surroundings.

Boys volunteer to live here. They're not orphans. They're not rejects. They've willingly left their families to work on intensely personal issues that have prevented them from being successful. Some have been victims of unfathomable abuse. Some have become addicted to drugs or pornography to escape the pain they feel. Others have inadvertently become addicted trying to fit in. A boy doesn't know how to deal with the death of his dad. Or a kid thinks he's worthless because his dad told him he wanted Mom to have an abortion rather than a son. They've punched holes in bedroom walls, gotten kicked out of school because they couldn't sit still, and contributed to the chaos going on around them.

These boys are some of the bravest young men I have ever encountered. At camp, they fight hard to overcome their struggles. Self-prescribed goals honed their focus as they seek to help the other nine boys with their goals, too. Every six weeks they return home to their families for a four-day weekend to put into practice what they've learned. Moms and step-dads and uncles and grandmothers—whoever the boys live with—also write personal goals to contribute to their individual family units. After their home visits, the boys return to camp to continue making the sometimes grueling, uphill climb toward success.

On average, it takes a boy a year and a half at camp to uncover and work through his trauma. There is no set time period; boys stay as long as it takes for them to be able to return home and participate in society successfully. During the boys' tenure three counselors, called chiefs, act like conductors in an orchestra. They guide the boys to work for the benefit of the group. They act as surrogate parents blowing noses and putting BandAids on cuts and teaching the older ones how to shave. They act as teachers devoting their time looking up words in the dictionary with their students or getting just as excited as the boys do when they chase after a black rat snake slithering down their trail.

They teach boys how to tie a hook on a fishing line or how to chop down a tree to be used for one of their cabins. Chiefs model appropriate ways to handle frustration or solve a problem. But there's even greatear opportunity to teach after a mistake. The counselors' goal is to empower the boys to achieve their goals.

I was blessed to be a counselor in the oldest group.

This is a story of a canoe trip toward the Atlantic Ocean. It began as a dream in our pine forest campsite and became a reality along rivers in middle Georgia. The boys took care of all the details: the food, equipment, our daily mileage, hospitals along the way—everything.

The group calculates gas mileage to and from their drop off and pick up points. Meals must meet dietary and budget requirements. All the boys must be proficient in basic first aid and Leave No Trace camping. Before big excursions, the group may practice river trip routines for a week on a river close to camp. They must know how to tie gear into canoes, set up tents, and start a fire using tinder from the surrounding area. Boys must learn to rely on their canoe partner to navigate the river. They write trip-specific goals such as learning how to stern (a stern is in the back of a canoe and is the driver), building trust, or investigating wildlife along the river.

Trips blend academic rigor with life-skills needed to be a positive influence in society. In a traditional school setting, students complete a project, turn it in, the teacher files it away, never to be seen again. Education at camp revolves around practical application of life-skills. When the folder is complete groupwork supervisors check it for safety and attainability. Then the supervisors return the folder with the charge of, "Go have fun!"

Boys make the most progress on trips. Survival, in their minds, is up to them. Dependence and character are not things to be talked about anymore; newfound virtues have to be acted upon to get to the destination downstream.

On the trip, they write articles for the camp newspaper. I asked that we keep a group journal. Each day one boy volunteered to jot down the day's experiences. This book is a culmination of my personal journal, the group journal, and some of the articles written on the longest canoe trip at Cameron Boys Camp.

Group Goals

We will explore and learn about the history around us by utilizing surrounding resources.

We will build a better group by encouraging and giving corrections as brothers.

We will keep a positive group spirit by depending on each other in the easy and difficult times.

Tyler

I will paddle consistently and encourage during the trip.

I will do two articles about the wildlife and what I see on the trip.

I will sacrifice for my group when needed and support all of the time.

Logan

I will learn more about the river by writing five facts a day.

I will keep small things small.

I will take "no" for an answer from my group.

Caleb

I will push myself and my group to fine-tune ourselves in taking the initiative and support.

I will do my best not to complain on the trip

I will complete two articles on the trip.

I will also get as much math done as possible.

Zach

I will get to know other people's stories.

I will respect chiefs and the group by listening to them.

I will learn more about trees and animals by writing two articles about them.

Chad

I will strive to pay attention by showing support consistently.

I will learn trip routines and other things about river trips.

I will improve my academics by writing four articles while on the trip.

Will

I will be flexible on what the group needs to do.

I will be vocal and help my group by volunteering for what needs to be done.

I will try to learn new things to write articles on.

Jaylen
I will help out my group by working hard when paddling and setting up camp.
I will respect my chiefs and group by not having the last word.
I will help the group by looking in the golden guides and sharing facts about the river.

Mitchell
I will have fun by doing whatever the group is doing.
I will be respectful by supporting whenever I can.
I will do two articles on wildlife and trip experiences.
I will read the book of James and tell what I learn to the group.

Robert
I will learn new things about nature.
I will be respectful to the group.
I will take "no" for an answer.
I will get to know the group better.

Chief Mike
I will remember the trip by journaling about each day of the river trip.
I will write one article for the Trail Talk.
I will share lots of stories with the group.
I will serve my co-chiefs.

Chief Jason
I will show encouragement and optimism all the time.
I will help empower my group and co-chiefs to take ownership of the trip.
I will journal every day.
I will read Luke and Judges (Ruth and I Samuel if finished).
I will do 85 consecutive pushups and 50 sit-ups every day.

Chief Travis
I will help my group by sharing my knowledge about canoeing and reading a river.
I will build spirit in my group by having fun and telling stories.
I will share more about the Bible with my group.
I will help and support my co-chiefs at all times.
I will remember my trip by journaling about my experiences.

Day I

Georgia on Our Minds

The first day of our river trip started at 4:00 a.m. A thunderstorm moved in last night at 12:30 a.m. that kept most of the boys awake. Storm or not, I was wide-eyed in excitement for my sophomore voyage on a long river. The boys were excited too. This adventure is what we have been planning for months. Before the boys left their tents, I grabbed trash bags from a storage box in our craft tent. With large, black trash bags over us no one complained of our makeshift raincoats as we made our way down the trail to the warehouse. Our raingear was already loaded in the trailer under mounds of food.

At the warehouse, we picked up our fresh food items from the refrigerator and checked the ties on the trailer that held our gear and canoes in place. Once everything was double-checked, we filled our Nalgene bottles and made sure our breakfast was in the van with us. We left a little later than our intended departure time of 5:00 a.m.

A few nights ago, I dreamt a friend was walking along a dry creek bed. I couldn't identify him. I only knew that he meant a lot to me. Behind him was an enormous snake. Its head was the size of a car tire, and its body was thick and short, like a pit viper. I yelled at the top of my lungs, but my friend couldn't hear me. I looked around, picked up rocks the size of basketballs, and hurled them toward the snake's head. They bounced off as the snake, unfazed, slithered closer to its prey. Only a few feet away, now the viper raised the front of its body into an S. Its fangs sank deep into my friend's chest over and over. There was nothing I could do. He died. I woke breathing heavily, trying to forget what just flashed through my mind.

My stomach gets a funny feeling when I forget something. I got that feeling right before we left the warehouse for Macon, Georgia. The drive took seven hours. Along with reading my book and replaying last night's dream, I talked with the boys. We stopped at a gas station to stretch our legs and fill up the tank. There we ran into an old chief named Rodney Doss. He didn't work at Cameron Boys Camp but had worked under Chief Mac, one of the founders of therapeutic camping. Seeing our trailer and noticing we stood in a circle, he made the correct assumption that we were a part of Chief Mac's camping legacy. He gave three "hows" with us. The audible "hows" stand for admiration, congradulation, and respect. It's also like our stamp of approval. We will also "how" throughout the day if we complete a plan and after the evaluation, feel like it was good enough to celebrate. He gave us his card so we could send pictures of our journey when we completed the trip.

In 1949, Chief Buford McKenzie (Chief Mac) joined Campbell Loughmiller at Camp Woodland Springs in Dallas, Texas. He began as a lifeguard. A few months later took on the role of a group chief. He spent four and a half years in the woods as a chief before becoming a groupwork supervisor. From there he served in numerous roles in Campbell Loughmiller-inspired camps all over the United States. These camps revolve around the philosophy of groups of ten boys and two or three chiefs solving problems together in an outdoor setting. The Eckerd Camps in Florida were started under Chief Mac's counsel. He was the director at Cameron Boys Camp at its opening in 1980 and stayed until his retirement on December 31, 1988. Chief Mac believed God called him to camp. God never called him away from his mission. After his retirement, we drove to his house down the road to sing Christmas carols to him and his wife, Lois. Sitting in his chair, he'd raise his hand to keep time and sing along. There'd always be time for stories. When we were with Chief Mac we knew we were in for a few stories of his camp adventures. Before we left, he'd shake everyone's hand, look them in the eye, and say, "You're special." And he meant it.

Near lunchtime, our bus and trailer pulled in a Wal-Mart parking lot to purchase fishing licenses for everyone over sixteen and to fill up our five-gallon water containers we call jerry jugs. The store's printer wasn't working, which nixed getting the licenses. In our search for water, we were directed to the garden department where an employee graciously let us use the hose. Several boys helped me haul the forty-pound jugs to the canoe trailer. We took another detour to Bass Pro Shop to get fishing licenses.

Later, in the heart of Georgia, after driving around in circles, we came to the conclusion that the put-in point on our map no longer existed. We asked a gentleman for directions. He pointed us toward a park he knew had a boat ramp. The park was eight miles above our original put-in that remained unfound. At a park by our new launch point, which I believe is Spring Street Landing, we gathered up under a mulberry tree.

While the chiefs stepped away for a brief moment to talk, some of the boys picked the berries and popped them in their mouths. Upon returning, I asked if they had eaten any of the poisonous berries. Eyes widened, and sprays of red berries came out of a few of their mouths. My smile showed almost immediately after I uttered "poisonous." They knew I was joking, but I hope they also understood the importance of checking with a chief before eating anything wild.

With leaving a little late and an unexpected stop to get fishing licenses, we launched our canoes at 4:30 p.m. Before we waved goodbye to Chief Brian, our supervisor and driver for the day, a man at the park told us that our put-in point was the terminus of the steamboat route. Upstream, the Ocmulgee River was considerably rockier, and even further upriver the Juliette Dam stopped all steam travel. Before we put our paddles in the water, we began work on our group goal of utilizing surrounding resources.

Despite our enthusiasm twelve hours earlier, morale was surprisingly low due to our late start. It affected our paddling. Logan and Will were canoe partners. Will doesn't do well when he's not in charge. I asked everyone to cluster the canoes together so we could discuss his unwillingness to listen to his partner. After the discussion, he turned his attitude around. I was shocked by how well he took the constructive criticism. Will has been at camp about six months and has made a lot of progress. He's introverted and superficial but defiant. Through his time at camp, he's beginning to soften and reveal more of his depth he's worked so hard to suppress.

I felt like we were moving slowly for the hour and a half we were on the river. We found a low lying sandbar on the right bank of the river that was to be our resting place for the night. The first thing we did after unloading canoes was team jobs. This is where the boys, in pairs, prepare for the evening. A pair cleans the canoes. Another constructs a latrine. Two pairs help with cooking: one pair cooks while the other sets

Team Job Rotation
- Canoes
- Casita
- Clean-up
- Cooks
- Pow-wow

out utensils, fills the water bottles, and other things to prepare for and clean up after the meal. The final group lays a small fire to be lit at pow-wow. Jobs switch when we reach our new campsite each day.

To clean the canoes, we let a small amount of water in the canoe by tipping it to one side slightly submerging one of the gunwales. Then we use our hands to scrub all the mud, leaves, and sand caked inside. To dump the water inside, we rock the canoe back and forth to get all the water moving in one direction with one boy at each end of the vessel. When the water moves to the middle of the canoe, both guys flip the canoe upside down quickly. The water, along with all the debris, falls out. Occasionally the boys miscalculate when the water reaches the center of the canoe. When this happens, one of them gets soaked when they flip the canoe. Today, Tyler, the more experienced camper, cleaned canoes with Chad. Chad lifted his end of the canoe too quickly. Tyler could see it coming, but there was nothing he could do. I watched from a distance, laughing. He was upset that his clothes were wet but didn't give Chad a hard time.

Cowboy Stew
White Bread
Ground Beef
Baked Beans
Canned Chili
Canned Corn
Dirt Cake
Oreos
Gummy Worms
Chocolate Pudding

Cowboy stew was on the menu along with dirt cake for dessert. Will ate dirt cake his first night at camp. Since then, he has tried to put dirt cake on every supper he makes. No complaints were heard with this meal. A few of the boy ate three helpings. This was one of the only menus we would have containing fresh meat.

The feeling I had back at camp rang true after dinner. We forgot toothpaste! I knew we were missing something but couldn't put my finger on it. We resorted to using hydrogen peroxide. Most of the guys were hesitant but all complied. Everyone's mouth was foaming as we brushed s teeth. For some, it appeared they looked rabid and intentionally made the foam come out of their mouths.

We made it to pow-wow around 8:30 p.m., which was great considering we reached our campsite at 6:00 p.m. Pow-wow is the last thing we do before going to bed, and we never end our day without one. One way we combat the chaos and negativity that surrounds almost every boys' home lives is to mine the good that happened during our nightly evaluation. Even if we have to stay up until one in the morning to get everything settled within the group, we'll still take time to do pow-wow before going to bed. While evaluating the day around a small fire, we talked about the generosity of the people who helped us today and the thankfulness of being on the river.

10:22 p.m.

I'm not really tired despite the early morning.

Group Journal: Day 1

Today we woke up at about 4:00 a.m. this morning. It was raining, so we wore trash bags to stay dry. After we had our rainy trail walk up to the warehouse, we started to pack up our fresh food and retied our trailer. Next we howed, and we started down to the put-in point on the river.

We had amazing academic time and we also talked a lot. We filled up on gas and stretched our legs. Our second time filling up, we met someone from an Eckerd camp. We howed with him, and we said goodbye. Next we had to go and get fishing licenses to go fishing on the river. That was Chief Jason's and my job. First we went to Wal-Mart but they needed photo identification which we did not all have. Instead we went to a place called Bass Pro Shop. It was an interesting place. Once we got our social security numbers for everyone that needed them, we got our fishing licenses. Now we left for our put-in point.

After about ten to fifteen minutes and asking directions, we came to a boat ramp nine miles above our put-in point. Once we got to our place to put in, we unloaded the trailer and unloaded canoes. We canoed to a wonderful campsite made of sand. We settled in for the night after pow-wow and a nice dinner made called cowboy stew. That was day one.

Caleb

Day II

Mitchell, the Hoister

It's our first full day! We missed getting on the river by four minutes. My goal is to get on the river by 9:00 a.m. every day. The average time for well-functioning groups to get on the river is 9:30 a.m. I want to set the standard a little higher for this group.

Loading canoes this morning was acceptable for a group without much experience. I know we'll get faster the long we're on the river. Everything we have must fit into our five canoes: tents, sleeping bags, cookery, food, clothes, water jugs, etc. It's an art maneuvering dry boxes and green duffle bags into the canoes.

After we get everything in position, we weave rope through the handles and on top of the boxes, securing them to the gunwales and seats. In case a canoe capsizes, we want our gear to remain inside. It's better to have wet gear than none at all. Some dry boxes weigh more than others. The weight inside the boxes can all be to one side making steering downstream difficult if loaded into a canoe the wrong way. We accidentally overloaded one canoe, which inevitably led to steering problems and hindered our advancement downstream.

We kept the same canoe partners from yesterday since we only canoed an hour and a half. Logan and Will had the heavy, lopsided canoe. Both became frustrated with each other when they couldn't keep the nose of the canoe downstream. They rattled off corrections to each other but were unwilling to work as a unit. Corrections often happen at camp. Sometimes they carry the venom of an attack because boys may use them to show another group member's faults. When giving and receiving corrections as friends, corrections are gentle guidance, like a soft "C" or "J" stroke that keeps a canoe on course. They're for the good of the entire canoe or entire group.

Still in the canoes, we gathered everyone up along the river's edge to discuss their attitudes a few times. Will's overwhelming desire to be in control, and Logan's sensitivity to adversity made the pair clash. While we talked, I told them they will become one of the reliable partners we will have before the trip ends. Logan rolled his eyes. Will looked away.

We ate lunch at a sandbar on the left side of the river. Nearby, I saw an old, worn set of stairs that rose from the river's edge. After lunch, we climbed the stairs to take a look around.

Ascending the steps, we found an abandoned field with a shack near the tree line. Weeds so tall that most were over our heads invaded the field. On the weeds were hundreds of cicada molts. They were also stuck to the bark of the surrounding trees. All of us were amazed by the concentration of the molts. We had never seen so many before. After making our way down the stairs, we put our trash in the black trash bag it came in, threw it in the bottom of a canoe, and went on our way.

We passed Warner-Robins Air Force Base today. It was on the right side of the river. Large planes flew low, directly overhead. The boys, Chief Travis, and I came to the conclusion there was only one plane. The aircraft seemed to be intentionally passing over us. We would watch it fly above us then wait ten or fifteen minutes and see one that looked the same go over again. I imagined the pilot trying to confuse or entertain the river-goers underneath. The boys thought they were special to have something so significant pay attention to them. One thing I did not want paying too much attention to our canoes were the three alligators we passed.

Alligators can snap a limb in an instant. Once pierced by dozens of teeth, alligators submerge in the water to drown their victims before their catch only saw one of the three. Different canoes spotted the others. All I saw was the head, but from the distance from its snout to its eyes, I estimated it was nine feet. It's been said that every inch between an alligator's eyes and its snout equals a foot of body length. I've seen alligators up close in a canoe before, but some of the boys haven't. A few tensed up. Their paddling slowed and their arms moved inward, hugging their bodies in the center of the canoe. I assured them that I was the scariest thing on the river and they need not fear.

The alligators weren't the only animal the group noticed. Tyler saw a dead boar in the brush, caught in an eddy on the left side of the river. We guessed it was three and a half feet long. The horrible smell repelled a few canoes, but I went over to take a look with my bowman. I was entertained by a few guys who put their shirts over their noses while trying to get their canoe partner to help them paddle away. One question the boys asked was if it had tusks. I rolled the boar with my paddle. Its face had decayed, so we had difficulty discerning if it had tusks.

Campsite tonight is on a large grassy area above the steep left bank of the river. We arrived after canoeing approximately five miles after lunch.

The struggle to get everything on land was fun for the boys once they committed to the task. Mitchell strapped a rope to his waist, and the boys in the canoes below tied the other end to the dry boxes. Once the boy at the riverbank gave the signal, Mitchell exploded into a sprint, attempting to hoist the box up. After getting so far, he looked like he was on a treadmill—his feet moving fast but his body going nowhere. Others went to Mitchell's aid to help him succeed.

Outside of camp, Mitchell doesn't have many friends. Others made fun of him because of his appearance or some other trivial reason. Mitchell never knew his dad. He passed away in a drunk-driving accident when Mitchell was an infant. Mitchell and his mom are unhealthily enmeshed. Mitchell takes full advantage of this. Mitchell's mom verbalizes her love often but has rarely taken steps to show it. Most days when the two are home, Mitchell sits in front of the television, and his mom has her nose in a book.

I enjoy when the boys come up with their own methods of pushing through difficulties. Some guidance was necessary with the dry boxes, but they took considerably more pride in their success because they were in control of solving the problem. We used Mitchell's system to get the remaining boxes to shore, not because it was the most efficient but because the boys bought into the plan. Mitchell was hailed a hero for his tactic.

While the cooks and I set out ingredients for the meal, the rest of the group explored around our campsite. Near the bank of the river, Chad caught a small water snake, his first snake. You could tell they found something as everyone jumped back. One of our boys is a snake guru and is always willing to lend a hand to include someone in his love of reptiles. Tyler, the snake charmer, identified the snake as a Northern Water Snake and helped Chad catch it after Chief Travis gave the okay. When the novelty of the woods wore out, the boys went fishing. Will caught a red belly sunfish. Tyler caught a catfish.

Over the fire preparing dinner, the cooks and I threw out the original plan of making pizza dodgers which would've involved getting sticks, shaving the bark off the end, and putting the dough around the debarked part of the stick. Then we would've had to hold the dough-laden stick over the coals until it cooked to a golden brown. After removing the stick and creating a pocket, we would have then put all the toppings inside to make a delicious meal. We had onions, green peppers, tomato sauce, cheese, and pepperoni. It's a time-consuming process, and if we didn't mix the dough to the right consistency, it wouldn't be able to hold its shape on the stick. But twilight was approaching so we opted to make a much faster, impromptu version of pizza dodgers. We called it pizza soup.

We mixed the powdered pizza dough packets with an excessive amount of water. We added all the other ingredients and stirred the pot. It turned out thick, but we went with it anyway. We would've been eating in the dark if we'd chosen to stay with the original meal. Everyone enjoyed the modification. It will probably turn into a rock in our stomachs. The ingredients at the bottom burned and stuck to the pot, which made cleaning terrible. Our steel scrubby was used for all its worth tonight. It was late by the time we finished cleaning.

At pow-wow, Logan and Will said they were glad to have gone through the difficulty of canoeing together. It made them better paddlers and created a bond only adversity can create. Tim Gibson, our camp director, said, "Group building is hindered by ideal situations." When problems arise, people come together. It's the same with this group; difficulties bring us closer. Even after one full day on the river, there seems to be truth to the prophecy.

10:23 p.m.

My goal for tomorrow is to make a lot of miles.

Group Journal: Day 2

Today we woke up and took down our tents. We did a good job moving out. After taking down tents we started to pack our canoes. That did not take long. Then we ate some awesome fruit stuff. It was good. When we were done we got on the river by about 9:04 a.m. That was good to hear. We saw a lot of cool things. One of those things was a dead boar. It smelled repulsive. I was amused by seeing the people's faces when they smelled the boar. Some of the other things the group had seen were three alligators. One was about nine feet long. The others were pretty big too, about five to six feet long.

Then, after that, it was time to have lunch. We stopped at this cool sandbar to eat. We had bologna sandwiches. They were so filling. When we were done eating we walked around the place we stopped to eat lunch. Where we went there were a lot of woods. There was an old house. That was awesome. After all that we got back in our canoes and made our way down the river. After about another five miles we found us a great campsite. When we got everything in their places and tent put up we went to do team jobs. It did not take us long. While we were doing that Tyler and Chad found a snake. Chad caught it. That was cool because it was the first snake Chad had ever caught.

After team jobs we did some fishing. Tyler and Will caught fish. Will caught a red belly sunfish and Tyler caught one bluegill and two catfish. The first catfish was not that big but the other one was about two pounds.

After a fun time fishing we stopped to eat some pizza. This pizza was like soup so we called it soup pizza. After that we went to pow-wow to end off our awesome day. I would have to say this was a good second day.

Logan

Day 2: What a Day

We popped out of bed, got dressed as quick as we could. Then we took down our tents. We did a good job moving out. Then after having fruit salad, we packed our canoes and headed down the river. By the time we got on the river it was about 9:04a.m. After canoeing about five miles, we saw something in the water. As we started to canoe over to it, we smelled something. It was a dead boar. Man, that thing smelled nasty! Then after looking at that for a bit, we went to have lunch. Lunch was bologna sandwiches. They were so good. When we were done, we got back on the river. It was time to find a campsite. When we did, we unpacked and put up tents. Then we ate and then went to pow-wow and bed. This was a good start to our trip.

Logan

New Adventures

It's 9:44 a.m. and right now we have just reached official Georgia and I look forward to the next three weeks here. And to be honest, everything is a lot different than North Carolina. A lot more buildings and way more plains and open fields than North Carolina. The minute we reached Georgia, I got so happy. I can't wait for canoeing. I can't say this enough. It's way different than Wake Forest.

I also enjoyed talking to my new best friend, Will. I'm definitely looking forward to the rest of this trip and how much more our group is going to learn and grow. I'm also excited about the cool fish and campsites we may have the opportunity to find. Also, like the article entitles, its name is new adventures, so be prepared to have fun.

It wasn't me, but Chad that caught a northern water snake commonly confused with a water moccasin. It's really cool how the group slowly but surely is changing as a group. Logan is having fun; learning by trying new things. Luckily for him the saying is, "practice makes perfect." So Tyler has successfully taught Chad how to catch a snake.

Chief Travis and I found a super cool campsite and this campsite was on a small cliff six feet up! It was cool since me and Chief Travis found it and it was super cool. I think the coolest part of today was while the group was canoeing Chief Jason told us he saw a boar. I have pictures that show today was the best day. I've had fun growing as a group and learning about each other.

Mitchell

Day Two on the Altamaha River

I just woke up and started to wonder what we will be doing that day. As soon as I started to wonder, Chief Jason said, "Time to get up." I got up, got dressed and got all my stuff out of my tent. When all that was done, me, Mitchell, and Chief Travis made fruit salad for breakfast. The vanilla pudding was real good.

After breakfast, we finished packing the canoe and checked over the ground. When all that was done, we got in the canoe. One thing I noticed was when it's cold outside, the water is warm. When it's hot outside, the water is cold. It was right after lunch time when I noticed a dead boar in the water. It smelled like crazy near it. After we canoed a little more downstream, we saw three alligators in the water.

That whole day we had airplanes go over our heads. The reason we saw airplanes was because there was an airbase close by. At the end of the day my group and I went fishing. I caught one red belly fish and Tyler caught two catfish. After pow-wow, I got in a gather up and hugged chiefs. I hope the next day is like today.

Will

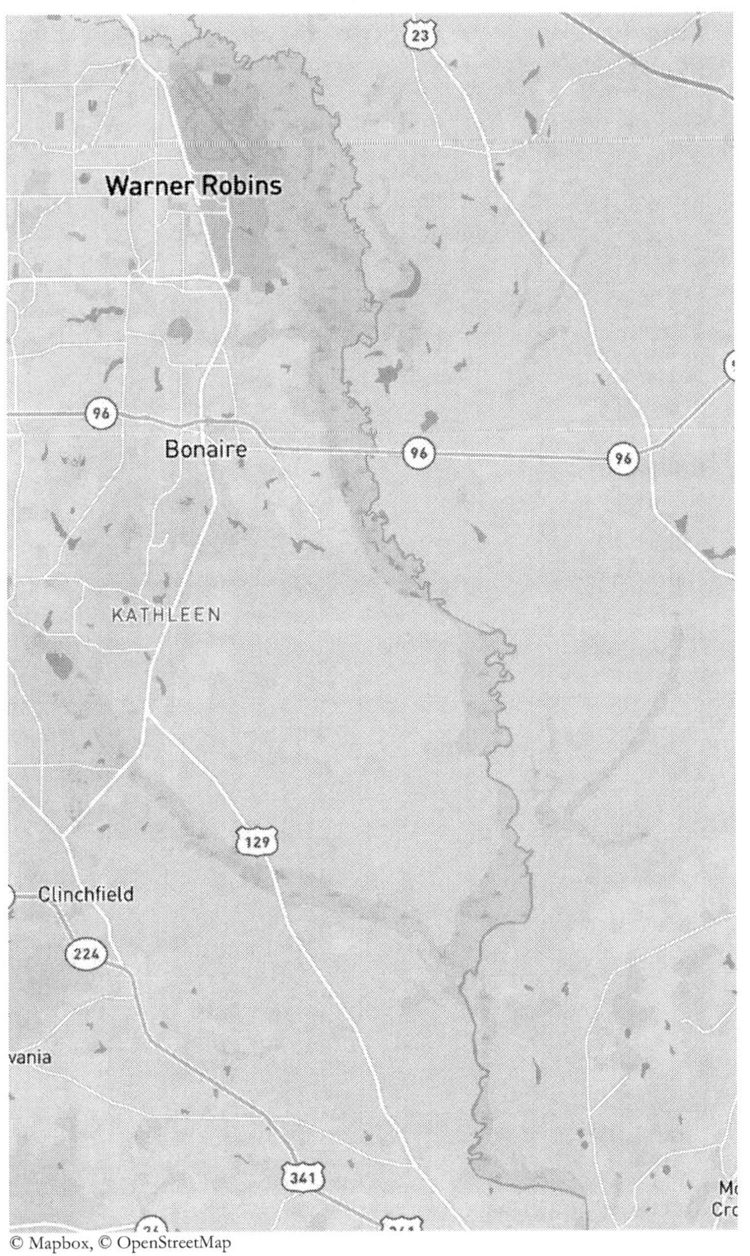
23
Warner Robins
96
Bonaire
96
96
KATHLEEN
129
Clinchfield
224
vania
341

Day III

Hangover Tree

We woke up to the sound of reveille from Warner Robins Air Force Base. It was light outside, and I was excited to get back on the river. After the boys woke up, got dressed, and packed up their sleeping pads and sleeping bags, they took down their three-man tents. All three boys worked together to accomplish this as efficiently as possible.

Logan and Chad folded the tent in half and then in half again, so it became a long narrow strip of material about a foot and a half wide. Then they folded the thin, slick rainfly to the same size and put it on top of the tarp. While they folded the tarp and rain fly, Robert unhooked the hollow metal poles that make the frame of the tent, sticking them in their designated bag. Robert picked up the tent stakes—six in total, one for each corner and one for the two sides. The tent stakes have their own bag. These two bags are set on top of the rainfly. Robert and Chad rolled everything into one big burrito. The burrito is stuffed into a final bag, which Logan held open, then put with the other tents in a dry box.

After these morning routines are complete, we evaluated how we did. Today we did well because we had good attitudes and were efficient with our time. If we do it quickly but fight with each other, we may set the tents back up and do it again. Doing things right trumps doing them quickly. We, then, say our goals to each other and move to cooking breakfast and loading the canoes.

Paddling with more skill, we made approximately nine miles before lunch. At Highway 96, I found a fisherman who was willing to drive me three miles to Bonaire to get water while the rest of the group ate lunch in the shade. I went to a gas station to fill up the depleted jerry jugs and to buy some much-needed toothpaste.

Halfway to the gas station, I realized I had not taken my debit card from my pack. I asked for the manager and told her my predicament, failing to mention I was representing a group of ten. She gave me a travel-size tube of toothpaste, not knowing I had nine others with me. I thankfully accepted her kind gesture and hopped back into the fisherman's cab. I didn't want to ask her for more since she was willing to give me something. While I was away, the rest of the group planned to ramble around the area and catch worms for fishing.

The canoes made several tight squeezes on the river with downed trees. Many of the trees still had green leaves. Fishermen told us tornadic storms blew recently all over the south. We were lucky to only see blue skies. My co-chief, Chief Travis, and I hypothesized with the group that these strong storms toppled them. He was the only other chief with me for the first part of the trip. Our other co-chief, Chief Mike, will join us on resupply. He went to Michigan for his sister's wedding.

Around 3:15 p.m., we found a campsite on a peninsula with several cypress trees. The peninsula was formed by a hairpin bend in the river. It is by far the coolest campsite yet on the trip, even rivaling the sites on a similar journey I took a year and a half ago down the Suwannee River in Florida.

Unloading canoes was fun with the slippery, clay embankment in-between the shore and campsite.

After unloading and setting our gear in a neat line, we did team jobs in preparation for our evening. We set up sticks and tinder for a pow-wow fire later tonight, gathered wood for cooking, and dug a hole for our toilet. Tonight, for canoe clean-up, we did something different than our regular team job. The bank was unfit to flip a canoe which meant the two partners needed to be in the water to clean the canoes. We had the canoe clean-up team help collect firewood until everyone else was done with their jobs. Today, cleaning canoes was an entire group endeavor.

Team Job Partners	
Caleb	Robert
Mitchell	Will
Tyler	Chad
Logan	Jaylen

Dressed in swimming suits, the group jumped into the murky water. We waterlogged the canoes and wiped the mud off the sides. It took three or four of us to turn a canoe upside down to let out all the water. Some of us struggled to keep our balance. Everyone could touch, but the clay underfoot kept it interesting. Jaylen's smile was contagious. He had so much fun cleaning and brought a joyous spirit to a job that could have been a nuisance. No one wanted to stop cleaning until the canoes were spotless.

When all the cleaned canoes were tied to a root or to each other, we bathed. After lathering up with green biodegradable soap, we jumped off a tree growing horizontally over the river. The river must have eroded the bank, widening its course and causing the mature tree to tip over. The current was strong. We tied ropes to the tree so, if needed, we could grab them before the current pulled us downstream. They dangled in the water unused.

All ten of us fit with ease on the outstretched tree. I wanted to take a group picture here. Right before the picture, Caleb ripped his swimsuit from the crotch all the way to the bottom of his suit. I didn't have to solicit any smiles from the group this time. He squeaked, "Chief! Chief! My suit ripped!" He had to lean against a branch so we could take an appropriate photo. Caleb didn't get embarrassed but chalked it up as a funny story he could tell when we got back. He'll have to wear boxers underneath his suit until resupply.

While cooks were preparing our meal, the rest wrote letters home or wrote articles about the first few days on the river. The boys wanted to fish while they wrote. Chad tied a hook to a spool of line, baited it with a worm, and tossed it into the current. He was excited to catch a fish with his rig, but a few minutes later, the spool slipped out of his hands into the water. Unfortunately, the spool unraveled in the water. Jaylen, Chad, and I managed to catch a piece of line that was tangled in the bushes.

Making a human chain so we wouldn't fall into the river we pulled as much of the line as we could. It was a knotted mess. Embarrassed that he had lost one of our only spools, Chad desperately tried to wind the line we had salvaged onto a stick during the rest of our academic time. He hoped it could be used again. We applauded him for his effort and told him that we'd be able to use what he saved.

Our focus was so concentrated on the fishing line and not falling into the river that we didn't notice one of the canoes floating away. The cooks noticed it on the other side of the hairpin curve. Chief Travis took one boy to retrieve the runaway canoe. They canoed out to it quickly, tying its front painter onto the rear of their canoe, towing it back to the rest of the fleet.

Tyler fell in this afternoon. The camera in his pocket was submerged in the plunge. Right now it's drying in a Ziplock bag of rice with my watch and camera that also got waterlogged. The rice is supposed to leech the water out. It has worked before, and hopefully, it'll work this time. Both of mine are supposed to be waterproof, but they've taken more than their share of bumps and falls. Unfortunately, Tyler's camera is not. I hope they work again.

With all the extra activities we did after we reached our peninsula, we still made it to pow-wow near 8:45 p.m.

Group Journal: Day 3

Today we woke up, got all of our sleeping bags, and started to take down our tents. After we took down our tents, our cooks made a good breakfast of scrambled pancakes for everyone. When we were done eating the delicious meal, we got all the canoes tied down and got in the canoes.

My canoe partner was Robert. I was stern and Robert was my bow. My group did around fifteen miles today. When we found a camp spot, we got all the dry boxes out on land, but we had to be careful because it was slippery. Oh! I almost forgot that on the river we saw an alligator on land. I thought that was awesome. Also, when we woke up that morning, the air base nearby was starting to get up as well. There was a song playing.

During lunchtime after all the paddling we did, there was a bridge. The first bridge I saw in a long time. On the other side of the bridge was a boating dock where we ate lunch. When we got out, we got in a gather-up, and Chief Jason grabbed the phone. When Chief Jason got back he told us that he was going to call camp's office, then he left. While he was gone everyone else ate lunch then went on a ramble to catch some worms for fishing.

Now that I have told you everything about that day I'm going to tell you about what we did after we found our campsite. Since we have not taken a shower in a long time, the group decided to take showers in the river. The water was not cold, so we decided to go swimming. Chief Jason got a rope and tied it to a tree. Then we got on the tree and jumped into the water. At the end of the day after we got dressed, we ate dinner and went to pow-wow. Pow-wow is where we end out the day with a good note. After pow-wow we got in a gather-up and hugged chiefs then went to bed. That was how our day three went.

Will

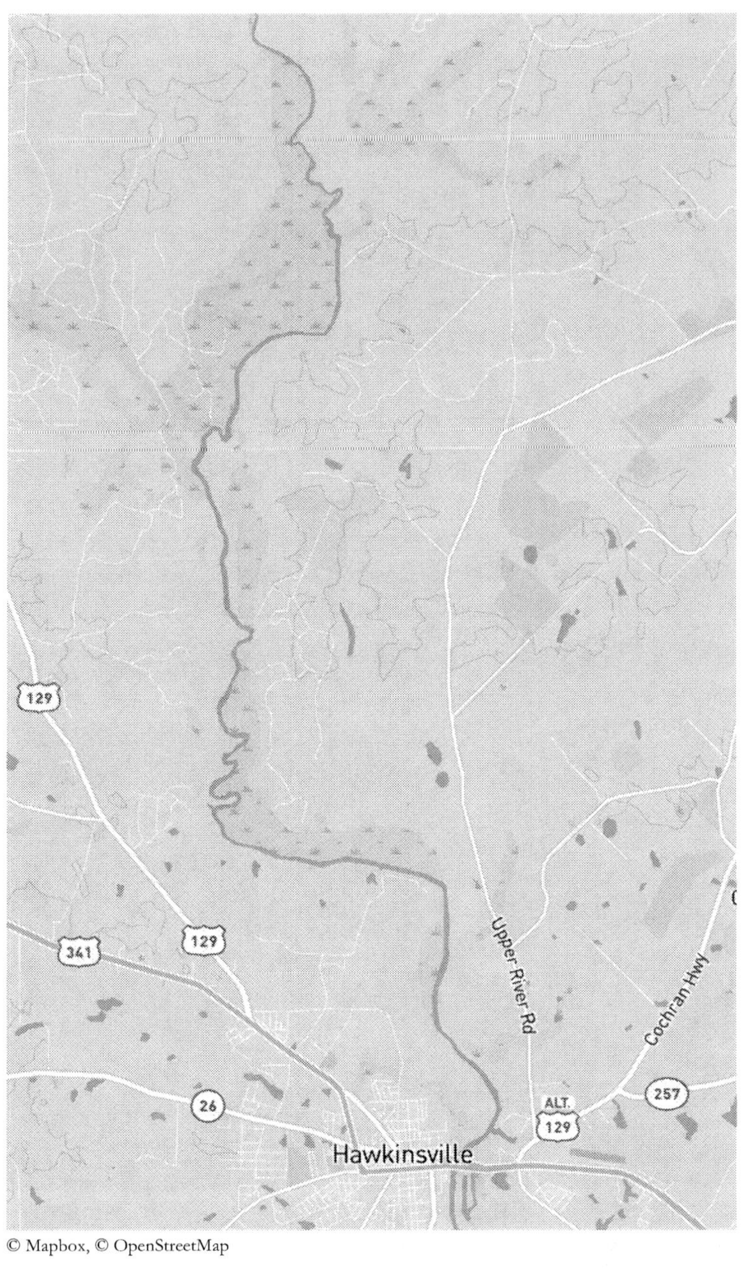
129
129
341
Upper River Rd
Cochran Hwy
257
26
ALT.
129
Hawkinsville

Day IV

Slippery Banks

I fell in the river twice today. The first happened when I was trying to return to shore after tying our equipment in the canoes this morning. The peninsula's steep banks warranted extra care to stay upright. When I finished tying the gear in the last canoe, I trusted a root with my full weight to pull myself up to campsite. As soon as I lifted off the wet clay embankment, I felt the root break. There was nothing I could do to stop myself as I splashed into the water. I saw the boys' heads peek over the bank waiting for my reaction. The root that broke was also the one holding the rope (called the painter) to a canoe. I was quick to grab hold and retie the canoe before it floated away. I was a little frustrated because I just changed into a fresh set of clothes the night before, but laughed it off. On trips we budget a set of clean clothes every three days.

The second was at our new campsite for the night tying canoes again. I slipped on the mud and rode the muddy bank ten feet to the water waving my hands frantically trying to keep my balance. This time I was caked in muck and didn't have a choice but to laugh. I'm sure everyone thought it was hilarious watching me try to catch my balance all the way to the water only to fall at the end. I'm already looking forward to a new change of clothes.

Floating downstream, we stayed in the canoes for lunch. Only the sterns had to guide the nose of the canoe with a few easy strokes. Some boys took off their shoes and let their feet skim the water. Trail mix was on the menu, so it was easy to pass out. The cooks mixed up lunch and put it into individual bags while breakfast cooked this morning. A little extra planning ahead helped us be efficient. We did stop briefly to fill our Nalgenes and relieve ourselves. But it was a five-minute stop verses a forty-minute stop.

I doubt our mileage, but the map says we canoed over twenty-five miles today. Our total mileage thus far is 58.2. It was a long day of paddling. Chad was my bow. We talked about music, food, and the zoo he wants to build. After attending North Carolina State, he told me he would like to find work at a zoo creating habitats for animals.

Chad is one of the brightest boys I have seen come into camp. He seems to retain everything put in front of him. He'll let you know how smart he is in a heartbeat. This frequently comes across as obnoxious and cocky. This spring, he told me that there were male and female pinecones. He emphatically let me know that all the pinecones we saw on the ground at camp were female. I didn't believe him at first, but we looked it up, and he was right. I don't think he intends to come across as a know-it-all; he just wants others to think he's important.

Chad's parents are divorced. He and his little brother live with their mom. His dad lives close by but doesn't take the initiative to do much with his two sons. Chad tries to seek his father's approval by spitting off facts and figures and by speaking loudly to get attention. His dad has duct-taped Chad's mouth to get him to shut up. To date, his dad has only written one letter to his son since Chad has been at camp. He came in July of last year.

Mitchell and Caleb were partners today. We put Mitchell in stern with Caleb at bow. Caleb has been on several canoe trips and knows how to steer a canoe. Chief Travis and I wanted him to teach Mitchell the basics of sterning. It was Mitchell's first voyage as the stern. Like a pinball hitting the sides of the machine, Mitchell's canoe bounced from bank to bank. This resulted in going under trees or crashing into bushes. Caleb would get a face full of branches when this happened. But he never gave up. Caleb vocalized his commitment to Mitchell frequently. Mitchell got frustrated with himself and rightly so. Going from bank to bank unable to control a canoe would test anyone's patience, but Caleb's encouragements helped keep Mitchell from blowing up. Caleb knew from experience that having a partner during times of trouble made everything more bearable.

Near the end of the day, I saw Mitchell scream and stab wildly at the bottom of his canoe. I thought he had become too exhausted from learning how to stern and snapped. He didn't say anything for a while. He must have been too scared to get words to come. I finally heard him scream, "SNAKE!"

I paddled over as quickly as I could. It must have fallen from one of the branches they went under. The serpent tried to make its way beneath one of the dry boxes to escape the frantic stabs of Mitchell's paddle. I noticed it was docile and assumed the bulge six inches from its head was a recently eaten meal. I'm sure Mitchell's decapitation attempts aided in it moving slowly too. It was a northern water snake. I picked it up with my paddle and put the one-and-a-half foot snake in the water.

If Mitchell could have hugged me from the other canoe, he would have. Fear was still present in his face as he moved back to his seat still breathing heavily. His eyes were wide, his face was as white as a ghost, but he knew the incident was over. He handled the situation impeccably, considering everything he was faced with. We switched Caleb and Tyler so Mitchell could relax. We didn't want to challenge him past his breaking point.

We are staying at Hawkinsville Park, a mile down from the Highway 341 Bridge. Chuck Sutherland, the park manager, let us stay for free, saving us fifteen dollars. He came back to our campsite and asked us to pick up pinecones in exchange for staying the night. The group thought his request was hilarious. The group gets plenty of practice living within a pine forest at camp. Cameron Boys Camp started in 1980, and the whole area was clear-cut to help fund the program. To restore vegetation, the camp staff planted thousands of pines in long rows. Now we use the timber to build our shelters in the three campsites. Among the towering pine rows are dogwood, sassafras, oak, and hickory. I didn't realize the pines were in rows until several months into living in the woods. At Hawkinsville Park, we picked enough pinecones to fill the two yellow barrels Mr. Sutherland left us in addition to two of our large trash bags.

I opened the bag of rice we put the wet electronics in yesterday. We needed the rice for tonight's enchilada pie. The rice was able to leech out the water in my camera and watch, but unfortunately, Tyler's camera was ruined. We'll save the memory card, and I told him I would put the rest of the pictures we will take on a CD so everyone can have them. He seemed lethargic when I told him about his camera's fate. "There's nothing I can do about it now anyway" was all he said. I reassured him that Chief Travis and I will take plenty of pictures and put them on CDs for the group.

I'm really enjoying this trip. The group is a bit rocky regarding their conversations in the canoes. Banter back and forth hasn't been degrading or immoral, but it's been teetering in the grey area and, unchecked, could quickly turn into a major issue in the group. There hasn't been as much depth as I would like. Hopefully, the group can turn itself around.

Tonight is the first night we have gotten to bed at a normal time. The first day we started late and wanted to canoe a while before pulling off. The second night we were trying to make up mileage we thought we missed the first day. Yesterday showers and swimming in the river set us back. One of the things I long to do is deepen my relationship with the boys. I came up with questions to ask in the canoes tomorrow. Maybe these will devour any negative conversations.

- What are your dreams?
- Who has made the biggest impact on you? Why?
- What do you want to do/who do you want to be when you grow up?
- If you could invent something, what would it be?
- What's your favorite restaurant?
- What do you love?
- What is your favorite Bible story?
- If you had a million dollars and had to give it away but couldn't give it away to anyone you knew, what would you do with it?

10:10 p.m.

Group Journal: Day 4

We woke up in the morning and left campsite later than normal and halfway through the river I saw a lot of good encouragement going on throughout canoes. I had a lot of fun with my canoe partner, Caleb. He didn't give up on me at all even though I was getting mad. But again, Caleb made me smile. He always makes me smile and laugh from time to time. I also had a very up close and personal confrontation with a water snake or a Northern Water Snake. It really freaked me out and I kind of took a swing at it, or more like a few swings. Well, after I took a few swings at the harmless water snake we switched bowsmen, and I was given Tyler, the funniest canoe partner I've had yet besides Chief Travis and Chief Jason. I didn't think me and Tyler had anything in common with each other but he said he would help me catch a snake, so I'm holding him to it. And I had a really fun time in the canoe with Chief Jason. He's really cool when you get to know him.

Mitchell

What a Snakey Day!

Good morning everybody! It's time to get dressed. Well, after we woke up, we moved out in tent jobs. After jobs we were told who our partners were. My canoe partner was Caleb. I was the stern. A stern is the driver of the canoe. A bow is the engine. Caleb was the engine for our canoe. Caleb is an awesome bowman, and since I'm still pretty new to sterning, I kind of messed up and ran us into a bunch of trees. Chief Jason heroically saved me after I screamed a little and took a few swings at the harmless recently fed brown water snake.

Halfway through the day, we switched canoes. My new bowman was Tyler. He was now my bow. Tyler and I said we would catch me a snake. However, we didn't catch one until later. Before I got there, we saw a lot of brown water snakes. Then Tyler caught a brown water snake right before we reached our last campsite.

Mitchell

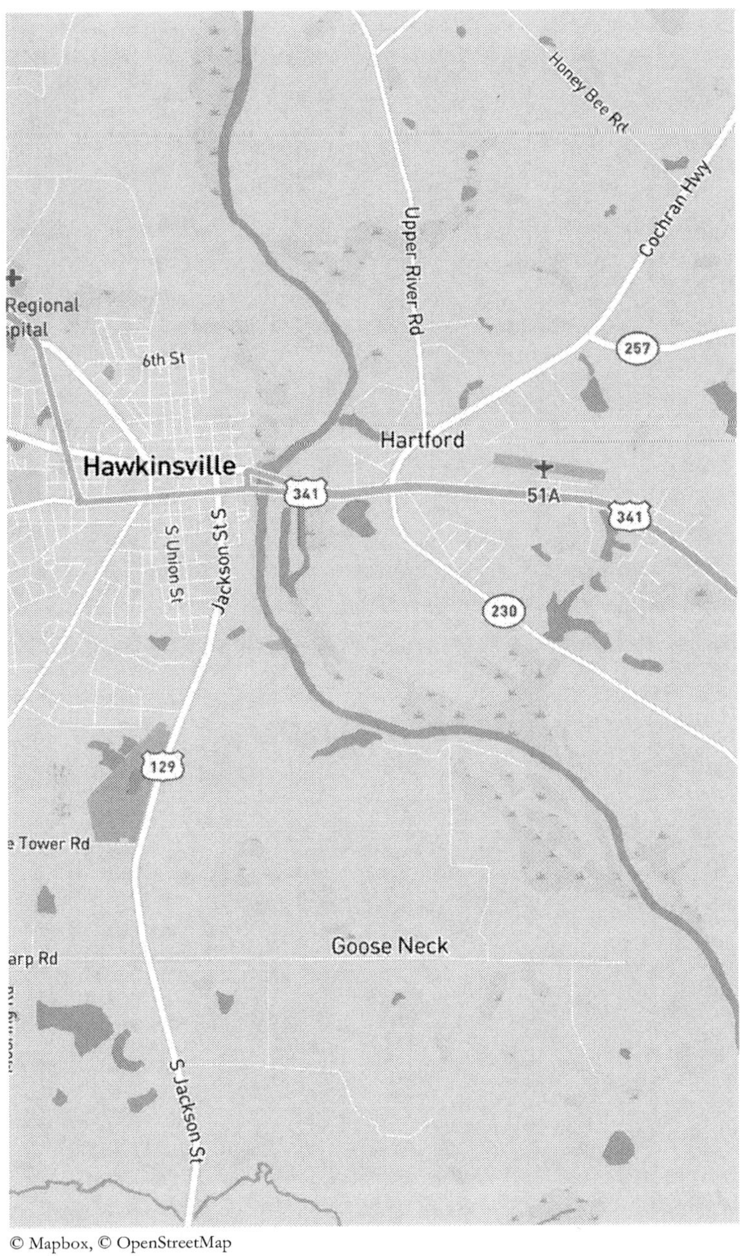

© Mapbox, © OpenStreetMap

Day V

Chris Bass

We woke up bright and early, stuffed our sleeping bags inside their stuff sacks, put our sleeping pads away, and rolled up our tents. I think we're starting to get the hang of morning routines. On the way to our destination, we saw a lot of turtles and alligators along the banks. The turtles are a lot more skittish than the alligators. Most of the time the rear canoes only see the skid marks in the sand where the turtles were. We also saw a few snakes wrapped around overhanging branches soaking up the sun's rays.

Singing and talking passed the time on the river, but our eyes never tired from trying to be the first to spot an animal. Caleb is a human radio. Songs are always bouncing around in his head which frequently make their way out of his mouth. Sometimes it's bothersome—he'll use it as a distraction to avoid thinking about what he needs to be engaged with. Today it lifted and unified our spirits.

Late this morning we were enjoying our time on the river. I was with Mitchell leading the four other canoes. We hugged the right side of the river. This morning Chief Travis and I asked Tyler to bow a canoe and help one of the other guys learn how to stern. The bow is at the front of the boat; it's the engine that propels the canoe. The bow also communicates to the stern if there are any rocks or fallen trees in the way. The stern is the steering wheel and adds extra thrust to the canoe.

Tyler's canoe was in the middle of the river when he saw a huge Diamondback Rattler on the left bank. He yelled, "SNAKE!" But this wasn't the sputtering terror with which Mitchell used the other day. This was a yell of excitement. Without hesitation, he began to canoe rapidly to what he thought was a huge venomous snake. I saw the snake too; it was the biggest I'd ever seen.

Instantly my mind flashed back to my dream. I knew it was going to be bad if he got close to the rattler. We were miles away from any professional help. I yelled over and over to stop, but he was locked in and paddling hard to shore. I was on the other side of the river but made a sharp turn and kept yelling. I did not want to take him to the hospital, nor did I want him to recklessly abandon the advice of an authority figure – a big reason he came to camp.

Paddling as hard as I could, I tried to get in-between Tyler and the snake. Tyler overpowered his stern. Mitchell was not giving me any powerful strokes from the bow. Nonetheless, we made it within five feet from Tyler's canoe, but it was too late. Just as I was in the process of lifting my paddle to throw at Tyler, we discovered the rattler was actually the tail of a large alligator.

By now neither canoe was paddling, but our momentum, even with paddles straight in the water acting as brakes, was sending us right into the alligator's path. The gator turned and retreated to the water directly toward our canoes. Did the alligator think we were a threat and was charging to attack? The first thing I could think of was to shove my paddle in the gator's mouth as soon as its head came above the gunwales. The alligator hit the side of our canoe as it slid into the water. Thankfully, I didn't have to ward off an attack.

As soon as I caught my breath, I gave Tyler a piece of my mind for refusing to listen. All of the canoes gathered together, and we talked about the ordeal. I was extremely thankful it wasn't a snake. Later, Mitchell expressed his terror when we canoed toward the diamondback. After his recent snake encounter he wanted nothing to do with snakes. He especially did not want to be anywhere near an alligator. I was so glad my dream didn't come true.

Around 2:00 p.m. we hit Sandy Hammock Boat Landing, fourteen miles away from Hawkinsville. The itinerary had us camping here tonight. There was a flat spot to camp with a gentle sloping shore, but I felt uneasy about staying. When Mitchell and I scoped out the area, we found some unhelpful characters using the area and girls strutting around in bikinis.

The boys already noticed the bikinis and wouldn't abate their gaze from the boat. This campsite would tempt my boys to return to vices they committed to abandon. Half the boys have experimented with marijuana, and at least three of the boys are sexually active. This planned stop was not going to become a reality. Some argued that we needed to stay here because they were tired and our itinerary marked this spot while trying to hide lustful eyes. Others didn't mind canoeing twelve more miles to the next landing.

The group bickered back and forth. Logan was one of the proponents of staying. He has not yet overcome his struggles with drugs and girls. It was evident today as he kept staring at a scant red bikini. Each way the group leaned sent more arguments into the air. Knowing this was not going to end well unless I did something quick, we made sure our canoes were onshore far enough to not float away. We walked down what looked like an old four-wheeler trail that ran adjacent to the river. Sometimes I need a walk to calm my nerves and process how I want to approach a situation. Walking also helps the group get their minds off arguing for a brief moment. This was my objective of this walk. When we stopped, we discussed the importance of being together and trusting chiefs. In the back of my mind, I knew without a shadow of a doubt that we will move on. I had to get my group behind me though. After letting everyone share their thoughts, we encouraged those who weren't talking or supporting to contribute to the conversation.

Eventually, everyone agreed to press on another twelve miles downstream. Tension was still thick in the air as some boys wrestled with right and wrong in their conscience. An old adage passed down from Chief Mac was if a group could sing together, they could do anything together. Before leaving the spot we held our discussion we sang, *You're My Brother* a few times. The motions that accompanied the singing brought smiles to everyone's faces. We ran back to the canoes to further encourage our newfound spirit and launched. Chief Travis and I rallied the group to make a wise decision without having to dictate by listening to everyone's opinion, being patient and speaking honestly about the situation in love.

You're My Brother[2]

You're my brother and my friend
You're my beginning and my end
You're all around me when the world turns and walks away –ay –ay
You're my sunshine on a cloudy day
You're the rain that washed my blues away
I can always count on you
Cuz you're my brother, you're my friend

Next came the long miles. I prayed our labor would not be in vain. The temperature was scorching, and the boys were tired. I encouraged the boys to keep going. Caleb began singing. Caleb is the camper who has been at camp the longest and is the only remaining camper to accompany me on the Suwannee River in August of 2009. On that trip, he was nicknamed Bumblebee. He had on a yellow lifejacket and a paddle to match, but what really earned him the name was his incessant singing. It reminded the boys who were on the Suwannee of Bumblebee from the first *Transformers* movie. Caleb knows almost all the camp songs. I can rely on him if I need help with a verse or need songs to compliment a certain theme.

Sometimes singing can be an unhealthy outlet for Caleb. He uses it to combat his loneliness and to distract himself from thinking about the issues he needs to deal with. A couple years ago, Caleb's father had a heart attack while playing softball and died on the field. As the oldest male in a family with four siblings, Caleb felt forced to take on a role that wasn't his to take. He started domineering his mother, trying to take the reigns as the authoritarian of the house. Neglecting himself was also a byproduct of attempting to run a house at such a young age. He was failing school when he came to camp and was physically aggressive to those who didn't listen to him. Today his singing was the perfect outlet for his tiredness and longing for group unity.

Finally, we reached Dodge County Public Boat Ramp to find several loud people occupying the shore. The landing looked characteristic to a little country town; lifted trucks, confederate tattoos, toothless smiles, and mullets, but no drugs or promiscuously-looking girls. The mosquitoes were absolutely horrible. I wanted to get started on routines quickly so no one would have a chance to complain. Luckily, we found a visually secluded area close by and began our routines with a sense of urgency. A late-night after canoeing so long would not set up our attitudes well for the next day.

Supper cooked quickly and was eaten just as fast. We sat in the midst of what seemed a spawning ground for mosquitoes. Most of the guys embraced them without too much slapping, but we all wanted to seek refuge in our tents as soon as possible. Surprisingly we did not get into campsite too late.

It only took two hours and thirty minutes to get the last twelve miles behind us. I am glad I trusted my gut and went for the campsite further down the river. We had enough time after supper to work on articles before calling it a night. The smoke from the cooking fire helped repel the mosquitoes, so we sat on the dry boxes near the smoldering coals.

While the boys were getting their pencils and clipboards out of our old ammunition can, a man from up the street stopped by and asked if we needed any firewood. A local with the characteristic mustache and twang of a southerner, he introduced himself as Chris Bass. We said we didn't need any firewood but asked him questions about the river. We knew from a placard at Hawkinsville that there were arrowheads along the river. We asked if he knew any information about them. With excitement, he replied that he did, then left on his golf cart. Upon returning a few minutes later, he opened a gallon-sized Ziplock bag with pristine arrowheads accompanied by stories of their retrieval. He went home after telling us a little more about the river.

We wanted to send him a thank you card for offering to give us any supplies we were lacking and also telling us about the arrowheads he found. Jaylen and I went to his house to get his address. In addition to his address, we also received a tour of his monstrous garage. We stopped him in the middle of the tour and asked if the rest of the group could be included.

With the entire group at Chris's home, he shared his hunting and fishing stories. A mounted boar he shot hung on the garage wall. It wouldn't fit on the deer scales at the butcher when they tried to weigh it. He and his buddies had to go to a grainery to use the vehicle scales. He left the boar in his truck, weighed the total, pushed out the boar to weigh the truck on its own, and then subtracted the difference. Another of his prize trophies was a hermaphrodite deer with hairy antlers. He said it was a three-in-a-million deer. Chris gave us some fishing gear before sending us away with a few good ol' redneck jokes.

Chatting with Mr. Bass made going to pow-wow later than we had expected. That didn't matter though. Taking time to talk with people we meet along the river makes the culture of the trip so much richer. It also helps us accomplish one of our group goals. Getting to bed later tonight wasn't due to wasting time or dealing with negative issues. Our extended night helped boost our trip experience. I'm glad we asked Chris questions instead of turning him politely away. None of that would have happened if we stayed at the other landing.

10:41 p.m.

We canoed twenty-six miles today.

Group Journal: Day 5

My day on the river was fun. We woke up this morning, took down tents, put our sleeping bags away, and gathered up. We had a very cool, tasty breakfast. It was beef jerky, pop tarts, and applesauce. Then we got on the river and did fourteen miles. On the way to our destination we saw a baby gator, turtles, and snakes. We saw a six-foot alligator lying on a bank. We traveled a good twenty-six miles today in the blazing hot sun. I think I got a little bit sunburnt but I'm okay; ready to keep going. We all sang songs and talked while going down the river. Everyone got to know each other on the river, and I think everyone is growing stronger as a group. We saw lots of funny birds fly over us as we were paddling down the river.

I can't wait for our new camper to join the group. He is going to have a ton of fun because being on the river really blows your mind. It's fun talking to my friend, Mitchell, and talking to Logan, and Caleb singing a lot. I want to welcome Zach into the group in a positive way, not in a negative way. I want to show him what to do and what not to do. At the end of the day, we found a loading dock, unloaded the boats, and found a campsite. There were a lot of people there but we got out of their way. After setting up tents and all the hard work, we ate dinner and had some very good conversations after we ate. Then we washed dishes and our hands, and gathered up. A man named Chris Bass showed us arrowheads and showed us things he had killed in the past and gave a camper a fishing hook. Then we went to pow-wow and hugged chiefs goodnight, and we all went to bed.

Robert

Amazing Day

"Hurry up guys, camp is just around the corner." That is what I heard on day five. We had done twenty-six miles that day, but I have to tell you about the beginning of that day for you to understand what I mean.

We woke up at Hawkinsville, Georgia. We were going to do fourteen miles. We heard about a boat landing that should be a pretty good spot to camp at. We paddled hard in raw anticipation to what our campsite will have in store for us. We ate lunch and stacked up on energy to keep paddling to our campsite. We reached campsite about forty-five minutes after lunch. We started untying our canoes when we noticed a problem in our group. We weren't supporting our group and we weren't trusting chiefs. We walked a little bit and we solved it pretty well. We then decided to go to a campsite twelve miles down the river.

We got there fairly quickly and we ate supper. After we ate supper, we came in contact with a guy named Chris Bass. He was an awesome guy. I hope we see more people like him because he showed us something he called southern hospitality and showed us some arrowheads. Then he showed us his house. He had a lot of deer antlers and heads. He also had turkey beards and claws. Then we saw his biggest one of all; a four-hundred and thirty pound boar! It was the biggest one I have ever seen.

After we saw all that we went to bed. It was really an awesome day full of fun, laughs and good problems that we were able to solve. I hope we have another one soon.

Caleb

Our Chance to Meet Chris Bass

We were on day five of our long river trip and after going to a campsite, we decided to go to another campsite. When we got to the other campsite, we met a guy named Chris Bass who said that he found some arrowheads along the river. After showing those to us, he invited us into his shed behind his house. When we got there the first things that we saw were deer heads and turkey beards. The first thing he did was give us fishing tackle and the next thing he did was show us his room where he kept his hunting trophies. He had one deer that had male and female traits. He also shot a hog that was too big for deer scales so he had to go to the cotton scales and weigh it. The boar in total was over four-hundred pounds.

After he showed us the place, we went back to campsite to head to bed. Chris Bass was a great person to talk to. He told us a lot of good stories and it's good that he was able to trust us to go into his shop behind his house and see some of the things he is proud of. He was a great person to talk to and get to know and I hope that we meet a whole lot more people like him while we're on the river trip.

Chad

Day VI

Jefferson

This morning we made an obstacle course on the river. The lead canoe maneuvered under trees near the bank. Just like the tree at the peninsula campsite, the earth under the trees had been cut out by the river. Trees bowed into the water; their branches made passageways. Some were wide and easy to pass through. Others had to be taken at just the right angle in order not to hit another branch ahead. A few times, we had to lean back, limboing under the branch to prevent being knocked out of the canoe.

Today would be a half layover day. We canoed seven miles to the Abbeville Landing before lunch. Already ahead of our mileage, we took time to explore when we reached the campsite. With our extra time, we explored the bank searching for arrowheads. Though we found dozens of wild hog tracks on the other side of the river, our search yielded no tangible reward, only mud on our clothes.

We played Stealth in the water near the landing with the dual purpose of washing off and cooling down. Stealth is like Marco Polo without calling back and forth to each other. One boy closes his eyes and tries to tag someone else. Everyone else can move around the designated playing area. If the boy who has his eyes closed goes underwater, no one can move until his head pops up again. The objective of the game is to be as quiet as you can. The current was strong today which made the game more challenging. We abandoned the game after a few rounds to walk along the jagged shoreline upstream, jump in, then float with our lifejackets on back to the landing. We did this until it lost its appeal.

We set up tents after playing in the river. Logan was given a simple correction by one of his tentmates. He began yelling wildly that he was working hard and that both his tentmates were the lazy ones. I gathered the group up to defuse the situation, but he wouldn't calm down. He refused to talk respectfully or lower his tone. He also didn't want to work on setting up his tent. The group suggested he sit by a tree to cool off and sort through his thoughts while we finished erecting the tents and started dinner. He listened because we implied he didn't have a choice. He could either fix what he needed to and help us, or sit by the tree. Plopped with his back against the tree Logan was huffing and puffing profanities while we continued with our evening routines.

His attitude didn't change by the time supper was ready, so I told him to stay by the tree. He assumed he could treat his group like trash and still eat with us like everything was okay. I let him know he could ask us to join him at any time, so he could talk about what made him so angry. During our meal, he called the group over. We abandoned our meal to join Logan. After a shallow apology that only addressed his outburst, we pressed him to go deeper.

Usually, if Logan is this upset at something as shallow as staying focused on the group, there is something more going on. After a few seconds of silence, he responded that he and Chad had undercurrent while canoeing together. The group defines undercurrent as something between boys that the chiefs or the entire group does not know about. It usually starts by singing unhelpful songs or talking about girls in inappropriate ways. It often devolves into ostracizing one of the other boys or a plot to run away. Logan and Chad's conversation involved girls. Tyler heard it earlier and said something to them but didn't relay his knowledge to the chiefs. Tyler's omission made me just as frustrated as Logan and Chad's conversation.

I normally don't have a fire behind my eyes, but I made it a point to set myself ablaze with this issue. I wanted to deter others from following the same path of talking about things they shouldn't, especially when they're in the canoe together. Undercurrent is the fastest way to rip a group to shreds.

Undercurrent will not happen in my group if I have any say about it. A chief has to be the defender of his group when no one else seems to be going for what is right. At times the group will push for laziness or chaos; the boys return to what they are comfortable with. Chaos at home is common, and the boys have learned to function within it. They even prefer it because they can see others stressed and hurt like they are. This morning, before leaving my sleeping bag, I prayed for problems. It may seem like an odd request, but without problems deep learning is hard to come by. These boys have a blessed opportunity to have problems in a safe environment where they are guided toward healthy responses. God sure has been answering prayer on this trip.

Earlier, a gentleman named Jimmy saw us struggling to push our tent stakes into the rocky ground. He brought down a hammer for us to use. He said he would pick it up later and drove away. I am glad the boys are getting to see southern hospitality with Chris Bass and now with Jimmy. I asked Jimmy if there were any educational/historical interest points in Abbeville. He said Jefferson made a trail through here and there are a statue and plaque about a half-mile up the road. I checked it out after the boys went to bed to get an idea of what it was before we took them.

On the way, I walked through a dirty southern town. Trash was scattered on the road and alongside ditches. Folks were on their porches, screaming at their chained dogs to quit barking at me. The youth were playing basketball on a court with weeds coming up from the cracks in the asphalt and a rusted chain for a net. When I got to the Jefferson statue which I estimated to be a mile into town I was shocked to find Jefferson Davis, not Thomas Jefferson. I was surprised, but I should have known better. I was in a small Georgian town.

When I got back to the landing, Jamie, another townsperson who lived up the road, was fishing with his wife. Reeling in a gar, he yelled at his wife to go fetch it for him. She screamed that she "ain't goin' in for no sharp-toothed gar." They bantered back and forth for a while before the fish broke the line.

Letting that situation die as quickly as it had come up, Jamie called me over. He asked if I could discern a deer print from a hog print and showed me how when I told him I couldn't. Deer prints are pointed; hog prints are rounded. I told him about our journey thus far and how special the boys are for wanting to embark on this trip and also work on their issues. Before he came to the landing, he had picked up a case of beer for the boys. It was in the dirty blue cooler in the bed of his truck. I am so glad he didn't offer it when the boys were awake.

Although we couldn't receive his offer, it was pretty cool that he wanted to welcome strangers with more than just a 'hello.' From his attire, I could tell he did not have much money nor was hygiene a high priority. This compounded his gift and reminded me of Jesus' parable of the woman who gave two mites[3]. Before I left, he told me again where he lived and told me to knock if we needed anything.

9:54 p.m.

Group Journal: Day 6

Hello guys. I am a fellow Ranger, and my name is Jaylen. Today we canoed seven miles from our campsite so that we could have a layover day since we are ahead of our miles. Today we also went through an obstacle course that was really hard for other people. Today we also got a chance to dig in the cliffs for some Indian artifacts so that we could have some fun. We also went swimming. When we went swimming, we played Marco Polo, and it was pretty fun.

Also, we cleaned out canoes, and it was pretty hard to do because the XL canoe was really heavy, and I almost fell in the water because the canoe was so heavy. We also found some hog tracks. When we went to go explore the river, I also saw a dead catfish head when we got stuck in the bushes. We also had a good meal yesterday that the cooks had made. We also had a good pow-wow because we ended off the day right so that we could start a new day. I also saw a lot of cypress on the river. We also solved a lot of problems yesterday. The group also learned that we should not have undercurrent in our group because it is not going to help out our group at all. We also set up campsite pretty quick so we could eat lunch because we were hungry Rangers.

Jaylen

Georgian People

The Georgian people are very nice. For instance, if you wave your hand at somebody, they will wave right back. Everybody down here is very happy to help out any way that they can.

Last night, we met a guy named Chris Bass at a public boat ramp. His house was the first one. After we got our canoes unpacked and our campsite put up, he came down just to check up on us to see if we needed any firewood or anything to start fire. We did not need any. Chief Jason asked for some history on the place and he told us that there used to be a lot of Indians. He showed us a lot of the arrowheads that he has found over the years. After we saw the arrowheads he took us to his house and showed us his animals that he has killed. And also let us try his turkey call.

It is cool to talk and learn about the people along the river in Georgia. So if you see somebody, talk. You never know what you'll find out.

Tyler

© Mapbox, © OpenStreetMap

Day VII

Big Fish

Some of the boys are missing the luxuries of camp and home. Fresh food is becoming the topic of more conversations. Boys are swapping mosquito stories or comparing how sore their arms are. It's starting to settle in that we will be on the river three more weeks. It didn't help that today was blistering hot. On the river, we don't get much relief from the sun. A few canoes got hung up on sandbars, but it didn't hinder the mileage we intended to make.

The boys' attitudes and support for each other faded throughout the day. If it doesn't improve on its own or through chiefs or a boy inspiring change, we will need to make a big issue of it tomorrow. At least there doesn't seem to be any more undercurrent. For me, issues that deteriorate the group are extremely important to fix early on. It will set the tone for the rest of the trip. It's the little things that have been happening today that have chipped away at our spirit. Most are repercussions of lethargy; not supporting chief or group members very much, a lack of encouragements and enthusiasm, and pessimistic conversations.

I also don't want Robert coming into the group thinking that camp is a place where the boys withhold from their chiefs or where sub-par standards permeate the group. Robert came into the group between the week-long Lumber River Trip and this one. Several homemade tattoos along his arms have slightly intimidated the other boys. He's about five feet, four inches tall and not fat but thick. His older brother, whom he looks up to, is supposedly in the Bloods.

Robert has been supportive and helpful on the trip, but too quiet. He hasn't been outright defiant to the chiefs or group members. When we've loaded or unloaded canoes, I can count on him to do his best; he works harder than most of the other boys. I want to bring him in the right way and let him settle into a good group. He'll grow much faster if he has healthy support by his side.

We saw the first mullets of the trip. They're small fish that frequently jump out of the water. They remind me of skipping rocks. They'll jump five or six times before hiding back under the water. Apparently, no one knows why they do this. We also saw mullets on the Suwannee River and read a plaque about them that didn't give us any answers as to why they jump. Today's entire journey was also accompanied by the music of millions of cicadas.

We made great time on our miles and reached a landing on the right about a mile and a half past Statham Shoals Boat Ramp by lunch. Our campsite is on the right side of the river on a sandbar. The sun made it unbearably hot. The guys who were not cooking found refuge under the trees. I watched Chief Travis and the cooks scramble in the heat waves radiating off the sand. As I read Judges with the guys working on articles or the journal, I was engulfed by sand fleas and gnats. I didn't mind the gnats too much because I had my bandana draped over my hat to keep them out of my ears. I had gotten used to them by now and didn't notice them crawling along the corners of my mouth and eyes. The fleas, however, I was able to feel. They were bigger than the gnats and were all over my arms and legs. I spent the remainder of my time flicking them off the pages of my book, constantly debating if I would rather take the heat or the bugs until the meal was ready. The boys with me were in the same predicament. We opted for the bugs.

During the evening, we worked on academics while fishing. We let a few of the guys leave their poles out for the night so they would have a better chance of catching something. Some of the boys used sticks to help secure their pole. Others just stuck the end of their pole in the sand.

While gathered in a circle getting a plan for pow-wow, a fish yanked one of the poles into the water. We were stunned, watching the event take place. The pole bent quickly, then fell completely over. It paused for a split second then got dragged into the water. We ran over too late to rescue it. The pole was Jaylen's. He was grinning ear to ear through his exaggerated lamentation, "Oh no, chief! I'm so mad I lost my pole. The fish must have been humongous to take it in the water that fast."

Lying has always been a habit for him. Kids didn't notice him much at school, and he didn't always get the attention he needed at home. Embellishing stories and turning to drugs were his coping mechanisms. He was glad to have something exciting happen to him tonight even if he lost his fishing pole. This time his story would be no fabrication. I was glad for him to receive attention that wasn't for something negative. I didn't mind too much about the pole; there's not much we can do about it now anyway.

It got up to ninety-four degrees today and is supposed to be hotter tomorrow. Several guys are sunburned but not too bad.

Group Journal: Day 7

We woke up this morning, and after getting things packed and having an amazing breakfast of blueberry and peanut butter scrambled pancakes, we finished packing and took bathroom breaks and then we were off. After canoeing a while, some people got stuck on sandbars, and some even got to see some weird fish called jumping mullets. Apparently no one knows why they jump out of the water. We've also seen a great amount of cicadas on the river.

We canoed to a boat ramp and ate a lunch of crackers, cheese, pepperoni, and dried pineapple with dried apples. After canoeing, we thought we found a campsite and we got really excited. Then we found out that it was too inhabited to stay there, so we pushed off and went off to find another campsite to officially stay at. Then we found a sandbar to stay at and we made campsite there. We have barbeque chicken for supper, and we hope it's really good.

We have really grown in the trip through goals and through pushing through problems. The great thing is we're able to solve them and put forth effort to make ourselves learn from our problems and make ourselves better through it all. We hope to learn more about rivers, wildlife on them, plants on them, and our session theme of plant and animal identification. We hope to also learn more about our canoe partners and how to better our canoeing skills to make ourselves more achievable on our goal of 300 miles on the river. This has been about day seven of the group journal for our long river trip. It is also about how it was building spirit with Robert while he was in my canoe by just singing and having fun as a group and as canoe partners. This was a really good day on the river trip.

Chad

Experiences

This morning I woke up, stuffed my sleeping bag and got in a gather-up and went on with our morning. Another camper and I started cooking breakfast for the group. We ate and started packing our boats and cleaning up our campsite. We put on our life jackets and grabbed our paddles and got in the water.

After 10 minutes of being on the water, I got super hot and started to sweat, so I drank some water and kept going. My partner Chad and I had fun talking about hunting and a lot of different foods we ate before camp. He was learning how to bow. After at least two hours, we stopped and had a very good lunch by a boat ramp.

After lunch, we got back on the water and after we paddled another good two or three hours. We found a good campsite. We got out of our boats, pulled them on land and began to unload. After unloading we started setting up tent and doing our team jobs. After that, we ate super good food, had very good talks, and got ready for pow-wow.

When pow-wow was over, we got in a gather up and hugged chiefs goodnight and went to bed. But before I went to sleep, I prayed and sat up most of the night just thinking about my parents and all the bad things I have done in the past and how I can make everything better for my family. Then I prayed again and fell asleep.

Robert

Day VIII

Creamy Chicken Alfredo

We woke up refreshed from sleeping on our soft sand mattresses. Chad and Tyler helped me fix breakfast. Luckily the sand wasn't melting our feet like it was when the cooks were preparing dinner last night. All three of us were thankful. When the bowls and spoons were cleaned, we helped the group finish loading our gear into the canoes. Today our voyage began at 8:48 a.m. We made it before 9:00 a.m.!

Shortly after Will and I put our paddles in the water we saw, up ahead, something swimming across the river. We put our paddles straight into the air motioning for the following canoes to keep quiet while we coasted toward the alligator. Everyone was surprised at how close we got to the modern dinosaur. We were within ten feet. Later, downstream, the same thing happened; the group saw another fairly large gator up close. We've seen a remarkable amount of wildlife on this trip: turtles, birds, snakes, alligators, and fish. It's helped the journey go a lot smoother, especially in the beginning. Usually, the boys will complain about paddling because they aren't used to consistently moving their arms back and forth for hours on end. Giving them a little break to take in the fauna has paid dividends in more ways than one.

For lunch, we rested on the left side of the river and walked up an old dirt road to a beautiful vista along a plateau. On our way up, we talked to a husband and wife who lived nearby. We asked about arrowheads around the area. They said there were burial grounds several miles up the road that had been looted over the last few months. It was too far for us to explore, so we remained on the plateau with our lunch. We began to roast in the sun, so we ate quickly then returned to the canoes.

The weather radio said temperatures would be in the mid-ninties today. Our sunscreen supply was running low, so we only put sunscreen on our arms and faces. For our legs, we put towels over them to shield them from the sun's rays.

By 3:00 p.m., we reached the steep landing of Mobly Bluff Boat Ramp in Ben Hill County Park. Camping was on a pay-by-honor system. I can't remember how much it cost, but it wasn't worth it at all. Climbing up the landing with all our gear would have taken an additional half-hour longer than usual. A sandbar at no cost one-hundred yards down the river caught our attention. We all quickly agreed to camp there instead.

Unloading the canoes took less than fourteen minutes. Setting up tents took longer than we planned, but we felt like we did our best. I did not agree, but sometimes I have to pick my battles. Jaylen and Logan set up their tent as fast as everyone else but argued the whole time. None of the three tents were set up as fast as they could have been.

The group went swimming following our team job routines. Chad, Jaylen, and I canoed our jerry jugs to the park to get filled. Both did a great job carrying them down the hill to the canoe. The three of us had forty-pound jugs in each hand. When we hit the shore of our campsite, the rest of the group yielded their game of Stealth to help carry jugs and put away the canoe. We still had time for the whole group to play in the water. It felt so good to have the group willing to help each other. That's what trips are about! The other boys knew Chad and Jaylen didn't get to play in the water as long as they did and wanted to help get as much fun time in for them as they could. Eight days into the trip and we're already seeing a group that's looking out for one another. The spirit has changed from yesterday.

Supper consisted of the best chicken alfredo I've had in a long time. Chief Travis created this menu. The fettuccini was cooked to perfection. It was drained with a little water left in the pot to make the sauce the right consistency. The canned chicken was tender. We couldn't say enough good things about the meal. I think the Velveeta made this meal shine more than the others. Chief Travis ordered an eight-ounce block to cut up, melt, and mix with the alfredo sauce.

Creamy Chicken Alfredo
Canned Chicken
Fettuccini
Alfredo Sauce
Velveeta Cheese
Italian Herb Seasoning
Canned Mandarin Oranges

Our evening plan of academic work was cut short by the swarms of gnats on the sandbar. Each guy had more gnats on him than a carcass would. Some boys retreated to the forest fifteen feet away, but beyond the tree-line, the mosquitoes took over. Everyone who attempted to get away from the gnats where engulfed. Their swarm rivaled the gnats.

During our shortened academic time, Logan and Jaylen asked to take down their tent and put it up again because they didn't do it with as good of an attitude as they could have. I sat next to them while they redid everything. As I eavesdropped, I overheard them talking about wanting to do better and having a good trip. Jaylen encouraged Logan to keep a good pace and to give it his all. Logan reminded Jaylen to stretch out the tent before putting the stakes in the ground. I loved it. They didn't need my help. The two of them had been arguing for days but seemed reconciled enough to take the initiative to set up their tent again all the way right. This was a breakthrough for both. They have such a difficult time admitting when they're wrong. Tonight they conquered their selfishness.

I was impressed with our support today. Robert chimed up more than usual. We had some minor problems, but a canoe trip isn't worth it if we don't face our issues and find ways to overcome them. Caleb's and Tyler's voices were heard consistently throughout the day. Support is one of Caleb's goals. It was good to see him work on it.

Caleb has been doing fairly well at camp. He's been here since December of 2008 but still has room to grow. He can discern between right and wrong but rarely acts on what he sees. "I will push myself and my group to fine-tune ourselves in taking the initiative and support" is a perfect goal for him. The oldest male in the house of three sisters and a brother, Caleb tries to be a father to his siblings. Becoming a leader by example, not a domineering dictator like he can be at home is something he is slowly growing into.

I'm excited to see change take place in his heart. He is also a big help to the others with routines and other camp specifics because he's been here so long, but too often he chooses to become reclusive rather than proactive with his knowledge. He's been on a long river trip before, so he's more comfortable during the long haul than most of the other boys. I'll definitely be pushing him to be chiefs' right-hand man with trip knowledge as the trip goes on.

During pow-wow, we heard three gunshots that sounded too close for comfort. A few minutes later, we saw a boat heading straight toward our campsite. No one was paying attention to the boy reading the plan for the next day. All eyes were on the boat. In the back of my mind, I was playing out different scenarios. Why were they coming this way? Were they running from something? Were they rednecks looking for trouble? Was this their property? How was I going to respond?

I moved between the group and the two figures, and acknowledged their presence with a smile and a wave. As the boat got closer, two young men said, "Hey! Do you want fresh catfish?" These first words melted all the boys' fear. They looked to me with wide eyes and asked, "Can we, Chief?" We gladly accepted.

All three fish had .22 bullet holes and were the cause of many "ohs" and "aws" from the boys. Each was between eight and ten pounds. We didn't eat them right away, but hid them in a dry box so no animal would bother them during the night. It looks like we'll have fish with breakfast in the morning.

There is no place I would rather be tonight.

Group Journal: Day 8

My journal entry.

Day Eight on the Ocmulgee River

"Time to get up!" "Sounds good, Chief." Well, that's how my day starts every morning. The only difference is that today we have lots to do. When Chief Jason said, "Time to get up," everybody jumped out of their sleeping bags and got dressed. Almost everyone got out of their tents in eight minutes. We got a plan for taking down tents in less than seven minutes and 30 seconds. The group finished our tents in five minutes.

Since everyone was doing so well, we decided to pack our canoes and eat breakfast. The cooks made some real good oatmeal that tasted like brown sugar. After breakfast we got in our canoes and canoed eighteen miles. When we were on the river, we saw a little blue heron and an alligator. Did you know a little blue heron lives in the south and eats insects? I also found out that an alligator mates from April to May after waking up from hibernation and it eats fresh meat.

After we canoed eighteen miles, we found a camp spot on a sandbar. When we pulled up, we got out and set up camp. After camp was set up, we got our bathing suits on and got in the water. The water felt like a pool. We played two games and they were Stealth and Marco Polo. It was fun. The last thing we did was articles. Everyone got a lot done. Before we went to bed that night, we did pow-wow. Everyone put in very well. After pow-wow we got in a gather up and hugged chiefs.

Will

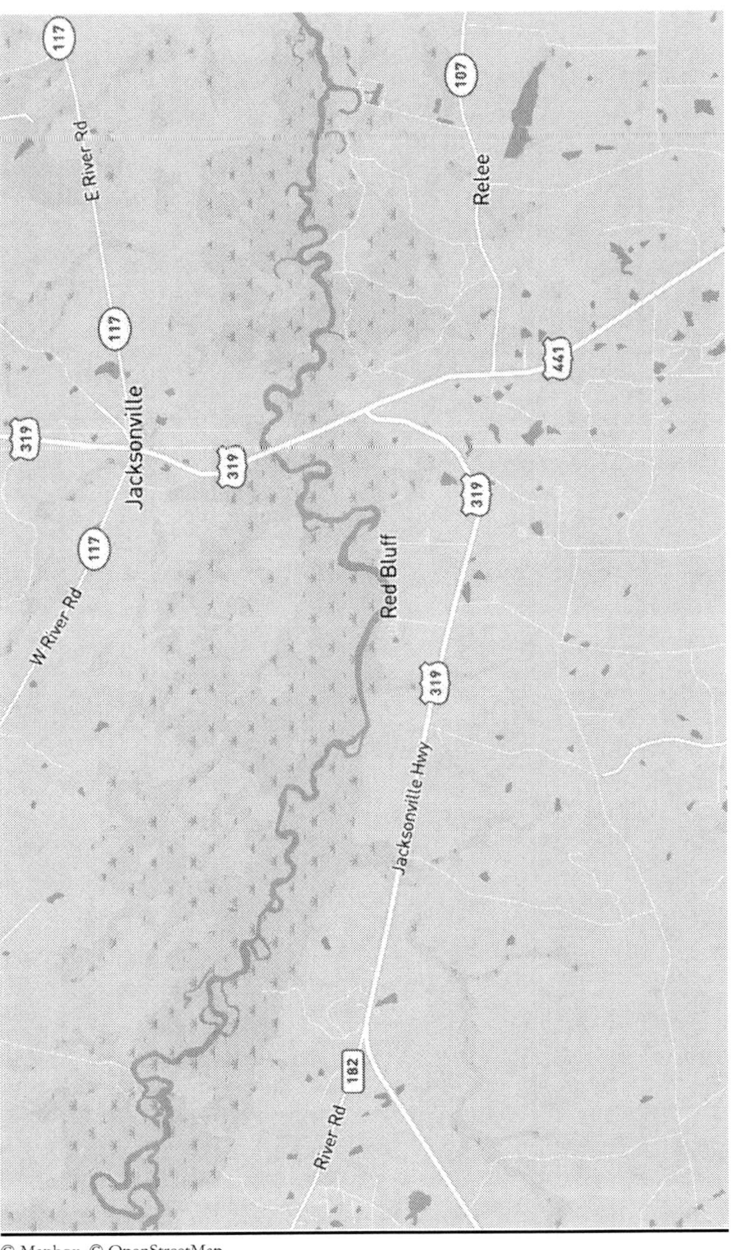

© Mapbox, © OpenStreetMap

Day IX

Slow Soft Shells

From the moment we unzipped our tents, the boys were arguing with each other. Jaylen and Mitchell didn't want to wake up. They moved like sloths putting their clothes on and getting out of their tents. Logan couldn't find his socks and began grumbling, refusing help from Chief Travis or me. Robert was slow and silent. He wasn't moving as quickly as he could have and he sure wasn't doing anything to help anyone else. Everyone seemed to get up on the wrong side of their sleeping bag. We also missed our time goal we set last night. With the lackluster attitudes damping our day, we decided to redo our waking up routines.

This meant redoing everything: putting sleeping bags and sleeping bags back into the tent, getting undressed, and then getting back into our sleeping bags. Even though it seemed petty, there wasn't much groaning. We had done this sort of thing at camp, and they knew the benefit of it. The purpose of redoing routines was to start the day with success. This early success helps set the tone for the entire day. When the boys woke up, got dressed, and stuffed their sleeping bags in a timely manner without arguing, we moved on to cooking breakfast and loading the canoes.

Another thing we did that was unusual besides doing waking up routines twice this morning was change into swimsuits. We planned on taking showers this afternoon and did not want to make another unneeded transition.

We ate the catfish the fishermen brought us last night. We flayed the catfish and put it on the grill grate we keep in one of the dry boxes. Elevating the grate, we made sure it would cook thoroughly but not burn. Texas Pete hot sauce and honey was all we found when we scrounged through our extra food. I've gotten used to Texas Pete; it's the only hot sauce that seems to be in North Carolina. Using all we had, we made a sweet and spicy glaze to put on some of the fish. It was amazing! God is taking care of us. Just the other day, we were dreaming of fresh food.

Today was another hot one. Everyone lathered their faces, necks, and arms with sunscreen. The boys were okay with draping towels over their legs again. We got the towels out of the army duffel bag, put on our lifejackets, and headed for the canoes with our partners.

Shortly after we launched from our campsite, we stopped at US-441 Bridge three miles down to replenish our sunscreen. This was also a perfect time to call camp and give the family workers a report on the boys. Chief Travis and Will succeeded in getting sunscreen, but there was no cell phone service to call camp. I tried two different carriers with the same result. I guess we'll have to wait until tomorrow to let camp know how we're doing.

While Chief Travis and Will were en route to the gas station, the rest played in the river under the bridge. There was a delta in the middle with the river dividing itself around it. This caused the current to become swift on each side of the island. We took advantage of the faster current by walking up the delta then floating back down. Several trucks honked or waved, giving us the illusion of being famous. The boys acknowledged the attention by smiling and waving back. We basked in the stardom while floating along waiting for Will and Chief Travis to return.

We wanted to paddle to Barr Bluff today. We saw it on the map but couldn't find it anywhere. We kept going and going in search of it. On the way, we saw a big soft-shell turtle on a long, shallow sandbar to the right. It was about two feet in diameter. We had seen evidence of them all along the river, but they always slid into the water before we saw them. Some of the boys thought they could catch it, and I let them correct their ignorance on their own. We pulled to the side of the bank sixty feet upstream from the turtle. I stayed in the canoe to watch. They didn't get within twenty-five feet before the turtle sprinted into the water, leaving the boys returning to the canoes with open mouths.

My laugh bellowed across the river as they made their way back to the fleet. Also on the way downstream, Tyler saw a long-nosed gar swim next to his canoe. He tried to touch it, but as soon as his fingers hit the water it swam away. Finally, we pulled off for the day at a pristine sandbar on the left side of the river. We never did find the bluffs.

Robert pushed everyone to unload quickly with his enthusiasm and encouragement. We untied the dry boxes and other items from the canoe and carried all of it fifty yards to the tree line of the sandbar. We completed the task in fifteen minutes. Robert was at a youth detention center and another residential care facility similar to ours. His older brother seems to be pulling Robert down the same destructive path. Robert came to camp for multiple stealing and fighting offenses as well as a defiant attitude. His personality inspires others to follow him. Whether he likes it or not, people in the group will follow his example, for good or ill. I hope we can get him rooted in following the right path at camp early.

At the campsite, we took showers in the river then swam. Some of the group tried to pick up a log from the bottom of the river lodged underneath sand and small stones. They would hold their breath and use all their might, but came up short every time. I gave it a try with them. There was no way we could get it up, but it entertained us.

I wanted to see if I could cross the river because some of the other boys wanted to search for arrowheads on the steep embankment on the other side. Thankfully I went alone. The current was deceptively strong. I struggled to get across and kept looking at the debris piled up checking for alligator eyes. I knew I wouldn't make it back without being swept downstream, so I climbed the loose rock and walked at least seventy-five feet upstream.

When I got in the water, I was immediately forced downstream. With all the debris and fallen trees, a few spear-like branches hid waiting for me under the water. I collided with a few and was fortunate not to get impaled or get my feet tangled. I covered the seventy-five-foot cushion in the time it took me to swim thirty feet across with all my strength. I told no one how much I struggled, but everyone saw I was out of breath and had scratches on my chest. We stayed close to the shore the rest of the time we were in the water.

We read through the trip journal during the evening meal. For some, it was intimidating to read their entry to the group, bad grammar and all. The group was patient and enjoyed hearing about our previous eight days. We laughed about Mitchell hoisting the dry boxes up the embankment and about Jaylen's marvelous catch that stole his pole. All of us shared mutual grief when one of the entries mentioned the swarms of mosquitoes.

The pair who built pow-wow added a little extra decoration tonight to compliment the view. We ended the day looking over a perfectly shaped palmetto leaf in front of the mighty river.

Group Journal: Day 9

This morning we got up and moved a little slow and didn't have a good attitude while doing tent jobs, so we had to redo waking up. We put our swimming trunks on since we were going to take showers this evening. After we paddled three miles, we stopped at a bridge. While Chief Travis and Will walked to the gas station to get some sunscreen and bug spray the group swam in the river until they got back.

We kept paddling hoping to find a place to do call-in, but we never did find a place. It got pretty hot today, so we had to put some towels over our legs so that we did not get burnt.

The group is starting to support more, so that is good. This afternoon we were pushing for time goals, and Robert really pushed for them. After setting up tents, we took showers and swam for a while. Some of us tried to get a rock up off the bottom but we never could get it up. Chief Travis took a lot of pictures of us playing in the water and we took one group picture.

I thought that was cool of Chief Jason to bring up a problem that did not get fixed from last night that I could fix it now. That is why I like the Ranger group because we do not do anything halfway.

We also found a big soft-shelled turtle. We tried to catch it but it ran into the water super fast. Before that, a long nosed gar swam close to our canoe. I tried to catch it but it swam in-between my fingers. Maybe I'll have better luck next time.

Tyler

My First Big River Trip

Once upon a time there was a group called the Rangers. The Rangers were canoeing the Ocmulgee and the Altamaha Rivers. When we were canoeing on the river, we saw some great blue herons. We also saw some alligators. While we were on the river, Tyler wanted to get up close to the alligator so that he could make me scared. We also saw a lot of snakes on the whole trip. We also saw a lot of fish jump out of the water while we were canoeing. Today Tyler almost caught a long nosed gar with his hands, but it moved too fast for him to catch.

We also had fun today because we went swimming, and we also took baths today so that we could smell good. We also explored some trees and bugs today. I also made a chiefs pow-wow, but Chief Travis messed it up with his foot so it became a foot-wow. Today we were fishing and hopefully we catch some fish because I want to hold them. I really like having fun with my group called the Rangers.

The reason why I am writing this article is because I love my group, the Rangers. This trip is really fun and I had a good time with the group. I also had fun with the group because we solved a lot of problems.

Jaylen

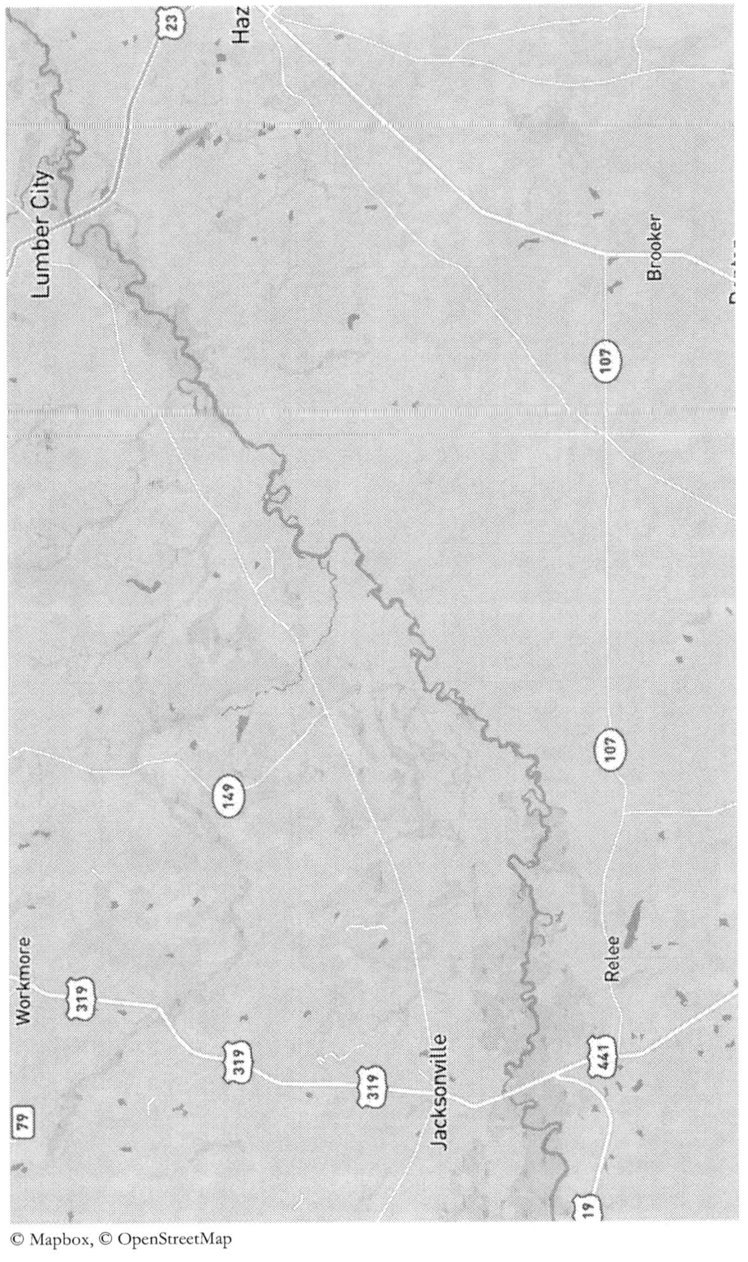

© Mapbox, © OpenStreetMap

Day X

Tumped

This morning we heard whip-poor-wills close to our campsite. They sang us to sleep last night. A good night's rest set us up for a great day. At breakfast, we finished reading through the first nine days of the trip as different boys recorded the days' events. Today was a layover day. We are blowing our mileage out of the water.

After our morning routines, we deep cleaned our gear. We washed all our lifejackets in the dry boxes with bleach then hung them on ropes strung between two trees. Sleeping bags were unzipped, hung, and Lysoled. Tents were bleached and Lysoled thoroughly. I can't tell if they smell, but I imagine they do. Sometimes my senses get used to the smell of sweat and body odor if I'm around it all the time.

When we finished cleaning this morning, we explored the land behind us. The group identified five new trees and learned more about the cicadas we keep seeing. The unbelievably loud hoards of cicadas were actually periodical cicadas, and their huge gatherings are more accurately defined as broods. These darkly camouflaged insects with golden wings lay their eggs on trees where the hatchlings burrow into the roots. There they feed and grow at a baffling rate; they take

Water Locust
Durand Oak
Sycamore
Winged Elm
Carolina Ash

either thirteen or seventeen years until they mature and are ready to resurface, mate, and die.

We learned this through our insect Audubon guide we brought along. Chad's investigative spirit was the driving force of our afternoon. He carried our Audubons throughout our ramble and asked dozens of questions. This helped pique the others' curiosities as well. He investigated a tree that had large thorns. Robert became inquisitive and, together, they looked it up in the tree Audubon. Chad also asked what the uses of the Durand Oak were. He knows about the white oak because we have some on the other side of the camp property that didn't get timbered before the pines were planted. He recited that the white oak was used for ship staves and whiskey barrels. We hypothesized for a few minutes while Caleb looked it up.

When the boys reached their focus limit for the ramble, we went swimming. Everyone enjoyed the cool water. When we got bored with swimming, a few boys helped me create an island. Last night we had pow-wow on a little peninsula. I wanted to see if we could dig a trench and turn the peninsula into an island. With some extra recruited help, we attempted our excavation project. We began using only our hands, then someone suggested that we use our e-tool, our lightweight, foldable mini-shovel. This was a brilliant idea.

While the e-tool made our island-making faster, it still took a long time. The sand would constantly cave in on itself, and we would be back to square one. But we were determined. The rest of the boys saw our plight and came over to lend a hand. The arc we had to make was about thirty feet, and by the time it was finished, the whole group had contributed.

Lunch was quick, and then we took a siesta in an oven. Our tents were so hot I felt like my arms were faucets; they kept dripping and dripping. I don't think anyone slept. We got up and went straight for the river to cool off before gathering up. Chief Travis and I felt cooling off was more important than following the normal routine. Afterward, we explored around a dried up flood-section of the Ocmulgee. The boys tried to catch frogs until they noticed they were stirring up clouds of mosquitoes near the stagnant water. Tyler found an oval-shaped egg the size of his thumb under a rotting log on our way back to the campsite. Chad and several others tried to look it up but were unable to identify the animal it belonged to.

Canoe Ball finished up our afternoon. It's a game where we partner up and get into an empty canoe. Once all the teams are in the water, one team receives a ball a little smaller than a volleyball with the objective of throwing it in one of the other canoes. The other canoes can block the throw with their paddles.

I was with Mitchell for this game. He asked if we could tump (capsize) our canoe because he saw some of the others do it. I told him that we better not. A few minutes later, when I reached for the ball, he seized the opportunity, leaned over the same way I was leaning and sent us both tumbling into the water. He hadn't tipped over yet and wanted to try it out. I reproached him with a smile, surprised he was bold enough to go through with it. I'm glad he was wise enough to purposely tump when there was nothing in the canoe. Capsizing a full canoe would have been a pain.

Supper went without a hitch. Following the meal, a few boys worked on articles about what we had seen so far, journals about the trip or letters to family members. Mitchell didn't want to do any of that and became disrespectful to the other guys. But he was really furious at himself. When confronted, he acknowledged he was angry with himself, but that he didn't care. The group wouldn't accept that he didn't care about himself. We were frustrated with him. We were angry so much had gone on in his life that he felt worthless.

His apathetic attitude stems from a long-enduring hatred toward himself. At times he's blamed himself for not having a dad…that he was so bad of a baby that he made his dad drink. At school, he let the lies that he's not good enough sink in. His confidence deflated, and he became antisocial, only spending time with his mom. Now they're enmeshed. He is all she has too. Mitchell needs to wean himself of total dependency of his mom. The group is also helping him look beyond a screen for fulfillment.

Sometimes, as chief, you have to stand up for a boy when he's unwilling or unable to stand up for himself. We fought hard to show Mitchell his worth, and the rest of the boys did too. The boys told brief stories of fun memories with Mitchell or how he had helped them. I think we helped establish some self-worth today or at least show him that he is worth a lot. The boys encouraged so well. No one can determine our self-worth. I cannot even determine my own self-worth. God has already determined it, and we're all incredibly valuable.

10:17 p.m.

I saw lightning a few minutes ago. Rain is almost imminent.

Group Journal: Day 10

This morning I woke up and heard some weird birds called whip-poor-wheels. Then the group woke up and cleaned out our tents. We got in a gather-up and took breaks. After that, the group split up and started to clean and cook breakfast.

During breakfast, we all had good conversations and read our group journal. We had a very big breakfast this morning. It was Slim Jims, oranges, rice, and beef jerky. After we ate, we split off again and started cleaning life jackets and made the fire bundle for pow-wow. Then the group went on a ramble to look up new things about cool things about trees.

After looking at trees, we all went back to campsite and found a spot to do academics. After that, we all went to our tents and went to sleep for about an hour. For about ten minutes I was trying to kill gnats by flicking them or smacking them on the tent but that really didn't work out so I went to sleep. I had a dream that it was raining turkey and ham and mac 'n cheese, but when I woke up it didn't come true. Thirty minutes later we all got out of tents and took a dip in the water. After that, we got in the boats and played canoe ball. Later on in the day we made supper. The rest of the day we went fishing and did more academics and went to pow-wow. Then we hugged chiefs goodnight and went to bed. The end.

Robert

Day 10: The Layover

Today I woke up not knowing that today was going to be so much fun. So I woke up and did tent jobs. Jaylen, my team job partner and I did a good job moving out. When we were done, the group got in a gather up and talked about how we did. Chiefs had some news for us. That news was that we were going to have a layover! Everyone got so happy when they heard that.

After we got the news, we did a few things. First we washed our life vests and sleeping bags. When all that was done, we did some exploring around. When we went exploring, we found some awesome things like a water locust tree that was cool. After doing some exploring, we did a little swimming. That was fun. Then after that we went to pow-wow to end off our awesome layover day. I would have to say that today was an awesome day.

Logan

Working on My Goals

My group just woke up when all of as sudden we heard a whippoorwill. It is one of my favorite sounds. When Chief Jason came in my tent, he told us to bring our sleeping bags out of our tents. After all that was done, we got in a gather up and Chief Jason told us we were going to have a layover. Then we split into two groups. My group (the cooks) got the meal out of the dry box and started the fire. When the fire was started, we filled a pot with water and then put it on the fire. Right when the water was boiling, Chief Travis poured the rice out on the sand. Only half got in the water.

After we cooked the food and ate it, we cleaned campsite, and got in a gather up. In the gather up, we decided to explore our campsite and we found a couple of cool trees. One was a water locust. It has thorns on it that looks like they were three inches long. Another tree was a sycamore tree. In the bible, Zacchaeus[4] was a small man who was a tax collector. He climbed the sycamore tree just to see Jesus. A sycamore tree is tall, so I wonder how Zacchaeus could climb it.

When we were done doing articles, we all decided to go swimming. That water was not cold. We played Marco Polo for about thirty minutes. Then we decided to dig a trench. The water flowed through the trench for about two minutes. Then the trench started to fall apart. After we finished swimming, we decided to eat lunch and then take a siesta. A siesta is where you relax and go to sleep. This siesta was different. It was hot. I was sweating like crazy.

We took a siesta for about thirty minutes and then chiefs came and woke us up. We were so hot, we decided to jump in the water and cool ourselves off. When we got out of the water, we rambled some more in the woods. Tyler, while we were rambling, found an egg. He thinks it's a snake egg. When we got done rambling in the woods, we decided to go fishing and do some more articles. Tyler caught a small brim. Right when I was going to do some fishing, cooks told us it was time for dinner. We had sweet and sour chicken, and it was good. After dinner, I finished my second article and fished for five minutes.

When we were done fishing and doing articles, we did pow-wow and bed. After pow-wow, we got in a gather up and hugged chiefs. Our group goal is, "The Rangers will explore our session theme of river plant and wildlife by utilizing resources and our golden guides while researching what we find." I think my group is working on this goal because every time we explore we bring our golden guides and look things up.

Will

Day XI

Storm

It looked like it was going to pour this morning, but we only got sprinkled on. We talked to a few fishermen as we were floating downriver and they told us to prepare for rain. We stopped in Lumber City to fill our jerry jugs. A man picked up Robert, Chad, and myself and drove us to a gas station. There I tried to call camp, but the cell phone wouldn't work. I used someone else's phone and left a message with Mom Lisa, our cook back at camp. There was no supervisor around to take the call. We are ahead of our mileage so we will be canoeing eighteen extra miles before our pick up at a new location. I'm thankful the gentleman picked us up. It would have been tiring to carry the jerry jugs all the way back to the boat landing.

At lunch, several of the boys tried sardines for the first time. I asked them all to, at least, taste it. The ones who have never tried them were intimidated by the can of fish. Will was one of the ones who had never tried sardines. Robert was the only one who couldn't stomach them. Many of them liked it after they overcame the idea of putting a whole fish in their mouths. I enjoy them; the smell doesn't bother me, especially on the river. While sitting on the left bank for lunch, we read a sign about the last raft that floated from here to Darien in the 1980s on a commemorative trip. We were close to McRae's Landing.

This evening looked as if a storm would bear down on us. First, Chief Travis and I had all the boys change into their swimsuits as to not get their regular clothes soaked. Then we secured all the tents by throwing ropes over them and tying the ropes to our filled jerry jugs that sat on either side of the tent. Chief Travis, Tyler, and Chad started a fire quickly and prepared our meal. The other group members and I set up a tarp to shield us from the rain while we ate.

The cool rain came as soon as we set up the big blue tarp, but the rain was not overbearing. Most of us stayed dry. Every so often, the canopy above us would fill up so much that it would overflow and splash the unsuspecting boys eating near the edge of the tarp. After the meal, the consistent rain turned into a drizzle then ceased altogether. The boys were able to get out paper and pencils to work on articles and letters before the night ended.

By the time we got a plan for pow-wow, we saw another storm front coming. This one looked worse than the first. We closed the day with three "hows." If we have consistently good plans throughout the day, we can choose to "how" after pow-wow. Immediately after the last "how," it started raining. This time the rain didn't let up. The wind grew more and more violent. Luckily the boys got into their tents quick enough to avoid getting soaked. In our own tent, Chief Travis and I prayed that the tents would stay secure in the sand with our makeshift braces.

All of a sudden, I felt my tent lift up. I rolled over to the side in the air in an attempt to keep the whole thing from rolling with us inside. Chief Travis moved close behind me to keep it on the ground. We looked out the window of the tent and saw third tent elevate like ours. I looked at Chief Travis and gave a simple nod; he was already thinking the same thing I was. We unzipped our tent and ran into the storm. I held third tent while Chief Travis held the chiefs' tent. While we embraced the torrent, I got out my camera to document the event. I took one picture of Chief Travis throughout the ordeal, but it turned out blurry. There was so much rain you could hardly see anything.

Logan's bag got soaked, and several of the guys are wet, but we are all safe. No one is complaining. A few of them even got their rain gear on and offered to help hold down the tents. Will was one of them.

Will had gone through several foster homes before being adopted into a loving family. Most of the foster homes were traumatic experiences. One foster mom physically abused him. He doesn't want to talk about it much. Because of the abuse, he harbors a deep abhorrence for women. He has a difficult time talking with Mrs. Kristin, his family worker at camp, and his relationship with his adoptive mom is terrible.

He shut off any emotional attachment with everyone. He just went through the motions to get his needs met. It was too painful to love anymore. This is one of the reasons he's at camp. We want to help him show genuine care for others and open himself up again. He's made progress with us, but it's going slower with his family.

He's a loveable, quiet kid who sometimes gets overlooked because he's not overtly defiant. I know he wants to be loved by the group. He longs to feel that the soothing effect of love which has been vacant for so many years. He's beginning to break through his fear to show others he cares. Sometimes we notice. I hope we have the wherewithal to notice more. Him, donned in rain gear, offering to help hold down tents in the rain was a huge breakthrough.

Deep down, all these guys will lay down their comforts to help their brother. This is what I love about camp; difficulties strengthen our group more than any ideal situation. Fifteen minutes later we saw remnants of blue sky that quickly turned to twilight. Third tent's poles were the only things that did not remain unscathed. They have an "S" shape to them now. I bent them back in place as best as I could.

When we were back in our tents, Chief Travis told me he thought he got struck by lightning when my camera's flash went off. We shared a few laughs reminiscing about the day. Right before bed, both of us heard a boat, and then saw its spotlight shine in our direction. We were already in for the night and didn't think much about it when we heard it sputter off.

9:42 p.m.

Group Journal: Day 11

Today I woke up to dark clouds lurking about my tent. It didn't rain last night like we thought it would, so I thought it would come today. Before breakfast, I checked my pole that I put out last night, and I had a catfish. My first one of the trip! Breakfast was freeze-dried scrambled eggs with bacon. It was super good! We cleaned up and packed up our canoes and waved bye to our home that had served us well for two days; no alligator bites at "Gator Island."

Tyler was my canoe partner, and we pushed off, looking to the dark blue and gray clouds above…a storm was coming. We passed a few fishermen that said rain was coming, so we were waiting. Finally, a cool breeze crept up on us as rain began to fall. This was it…or so we thought. The clouds soon broke, and the sun came shining out to dry and warm our recently chilled bodies. Tyler and I led the group with a good pace, and we soon found a landing with a man skinning a catfish. We now knew where we were and headed off to end the day at Hard Bargain Landing

The day was back to overcast when we stopped for lunch at McRae's Landing and read about the last raft trip on the Ocmulgee and Altamaha. This was also our sardine meal. Surprisingly everyone enjoyed them except for Robert. We got back on the river and paddled until we got to the bridge. Chief Jason, Robert, and Chad went to get water and were picked up by some nice people. I stayed with the group, and we explored the railroad and found railroad ties that came in handy later. We also found a huge turtle. He peed on Logan.

Alas, we made it to camp, and it was still beautiful. Just as we started making dinner, we saw a storm rolling in. Tyler, Chad, and I quickly made dinner while the others put up a tent that we could eat under. This storm was not going to miss us this time. As we were about to walk to the tarp to eat, we all stopped to watch in awe at the storm. We could see the rain that was about to dump on us inching closer. Just as we got under the tarp, the rain came. The rain stopped as we cleaned up and did academics. We worked hard and got things done. As we were about to go to pow-wow, we saw another storm coming. It hit as pow-wow came to a close. We all scurried to our tents and got in. Chief Jason and I were watching the wind pick up. Then our tent started bending. While we were holding ours from the inside, third tent lifted off, and the two heroic chiefs were out in the storm battling nature! The hurricane lasted about ten minutes. We tried to put everything back, but it was all wet and sandy. Words don't do it justice, but this night will not soon be forgotten.

Chief Travis

The Storm That Rocked Our Campsite

"We are going to die!" first tent exclaimed. During this, the worst storm that I've ever been through was going on outside. But before I tell you that, I must tell you this.

We were on day eleven of our long river trip. Some fishermen we were talking to said that it called for severe thunderstorms. We canoed the whole day under a sunny sky and got to campsite. Once we were eating dinner, it started. It was a slow, steady beating rain. It quit for pow-wow. For sleeping, however, we weren't as fortunate.

Lightning flashing, thunder rolling and tents trying to fly away just added to the chaos caused by the storm. The fact that tents were flying away meant that some people were not sleeping very well. Our sleeping bags were also very soaked and it was a very wet night along with the sand in your feet getting all in your sleeping bag. This was a huge storm for us to sleep in, and I doubt we'll forget about this anytime soon. This was so much fun and I hope this happens to us again at least once while on our trip.

Chad

Reptiles on the River

So far on the trip we have seen plenty of reptiles; mostly they have been alligators, brown water snakes, and many sorts of turtles. All of them have been basking in the sun. This really isn't a surprise to most people because all reptiles are cold blooded and basking in the sun is the way to warm their blood up.

The alligators can get up to nineteen and a half feet long. But the biggest one that we have seen was about eight feet long. We read online before we went on our trip about the brown water snakes falling out of trees on people, and we got to encounter one falling into Mitchell and Caleb's canoe. Luckily Chief Jason could get the snake out of the canoe safely. Most people don't like snakes at all. However, if they will look them up and find something cool about them and why they live, maybe they will change their thoughts.

We have seen a lot of turtles lying on logs, but if we even try to get close to them, they will jump off and swim away, but today Logan and I found a turtle lying on the sand. He caught it and the group looked and studied it and learned that it was a yellow bellied slider.

Tyler

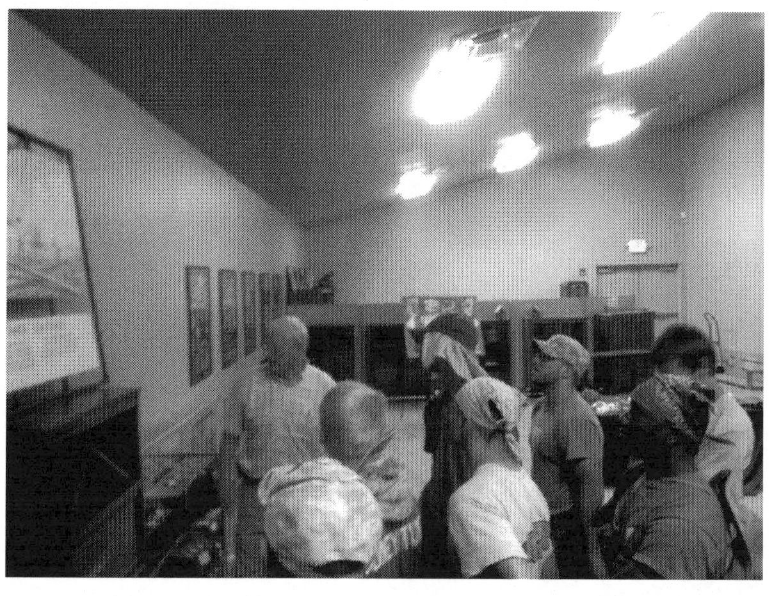

Day XII

Visit with Mr. Bill

At breakfast, we all recounted the storm that bore down on us last night. I told the group about chief's tent being lifted and Chief Travis and I looking at each other with game faces on ready to embrace the storm. We all laughed when Chief Travis told of his near-death lightning experience that turned out to be my camera flash. We thanked everyone who was willing to help and also those who were wet, for not complaining.

Logan piped up and recounted his experience from third tent last night while we were still seated in a circle eating breakfast. During the storm, he was terrified by the wind and rain. He prayed that someone would save him as he was bracing the tent from the inside. At that moment, he felt a hand grab his and told us that God sent him a guardian angel. I continued with his story, telling the group I had inadvertently grabbed his hand when I was holding the tent from the outside. We all laughed as Logan realized his guardian angel was really me. I told them that sometimes, God uses us to answer prayers.

In-between the meal and packing up the canoes for our daily voyage, a friendly man in a johnboat drove over to us. He told us he was the one who had checked on us last night and made sure our tents were still standing. He was surprised we made it through with only a few bent poles and said he would have come ashore and gotten us to safety if the storm had lasted any longer. We thanked him for checking on us. The boys are noticing that God has been protecting us on the river and sending people to check on us.

While canoeing this morning, we saw a speedboat. The boat hardly made a wake. When the driver hit the throttle, it lunged out of the water at rocket speed. It didn't go more than twenty seconds before it had to stop and turn around. The group coasted for a while looking at it with their jaws on the bottom of the canoe. I couldn't count how many times the boat circled us. Whoever it was must have a lot of money to be doing that.

We stopped at Towns Bluff Landing today, where we met Mr. Bill, one of the landing's employees. He walked us through the museum and told us about rafting on the Altamaha. Rafting, he said, preceded steamboats. Two men would guide a two-hundred-foot by fifty-foot raft from here all the way to Darien! The river has changed a lot since then, but it is almost unfathomable to think of those big rafts floating down the same river we are. Mr. Bill said the raftsmen knew the river so well they knew every bend in the river by name. Most of the men walked back after their raft reached its destination only to do it all over again. Their rafts were broken apart at the coast and shipped to England or the West Indies as timber.

After listening to river history from Mr. Bill, we walked around the park in search of a monster cypress tree he told us about. We searched and searched but left without finding it. We will have to find it next time we come. We are so ahead of our mileage that we switched our resupply destination. At resupply, one of the supervisors will come with a van and canoe trailer. We'll load everything up on the trailer and will drive to the Oconee River, another tributary of the Altamaha. At the rate we are going, we would have run into the ocean days before we were supposed to be picked up if we hadn't modified our itinerary.

We left the park after 3:00 p.m. and took our time down the river. On the left side, we saw the remains of an old steamboat boiler Mr. Bill had mentioned earlier this afternoon. Steamboats, back in the 1800s, would drag race down the river. Captains would overheat the boilers, and occasionally the boilers would explode sending fragments of metal everywhere. We imagined the fiery scene that took place at this spot long ago.

9:53 p.m.

Our campsite tonight is on a big sandbar on the right side of the river.

Group Journal: Day 12

Good morning everybody. It's time to wake up and move out in tent and team jobs. We have to move out in the morning so we get to paddling on the Altamaha. After we woke up, moved out, got sunscreen on, we were told our canoe partners. For the first time my partner was Robert. I definitely learned a lot about him like what he likes to do when he's by himself or with friends, or just BMXing or riding dirt bikes. I also learned what his favorite place to eat is: Subway. Once we were done talking about him and his life we arrived at a bridge, and there we saw an awesome super really sweet boat, a speed boat to be precise. It was showing off and speeding in the water for us. Me and Robert had never seen a speed boat before in real life except on TV. It was so much fun getting to know Robert. He's a really awesome guy once to get to know him. To be honest, I'm glad I was his canoe partner today. I learned about Robert.

Mitchell

My Canoe Partner, Robert

This morning we woke up and moved out in tent jobs. We ate an amazing meal, which was breakfast, and then after we ate, we had an awesome conversation. Then we were told who our canoe partners were going to be. I was hoping my partner would be Robert because that guy is teaching me about dirt bikes and four wheelers. Since I still don't know all about four wheelers, he said he would tell me more.

Also we've been trying to make up a song together. Right now we've got two songs so far, and we hope to get more songs done. Also while I was in a canoe with Robert, we saw a guy in a really sweet looking speed boat. He must have been a professional at speed racing because he was flying around us really fast. That was a cool experience because I've never seen a speed boat before. Robert and I both thought that was really cool. That's the same day we saw a huge stuffed boar. That was a cool day with Robert.

Mitchell

Adventures

Today was one of the best days of my life. This morning we woke up after a bad storm last night and got soaked. We woke up, cleaned out our tents, and then got in a gather up. After that we ate breakfast and put on our life jackets and grabbed our paddles. Next we checked our campsite for any trash or just anything that's left that we did not get. After scanning camp, we found out who our boat partners were. My partner was my friend, Mitchell. We didn't really know a lot about each other, so I couldn't wait to learn about him. Then we got in our boats and began our day on the river. When we started paddling, I asked Mitchell about his life and about his favorite foods and drinks.

Later in the day, I found out about his family and what he liked to do for fun. He told me that he always wanted an ATV or a dirt bike, but I told him that he would get one someday. Mitchell and I sang some songs going down the river and we really got to know each other. I thought I would never meet someone like Mitchell till I came to camp and met the rest of the group and the chiefs.

The camp I'm at is really fun. Also, today I saw my first speed boat and we got to know and see some really cool things that were on the river long ago. I met some really cool people and had a good lunch. Then we went on a little nature walk. But my best part of the day was going to pow-wow and to bed. Before I go to bed, I pray and then I go to bed.

Robert

Boating Evolution on the River

I learned how boats have evolved over time from a guy named Mr. Bill. He told us some history of boats. In the late 1800s, they would build huge rafts and take them down the river. These rafts would be made out of yellow pine. Lumberjacks would chop down trees and then square the logs. It was like notching a whole log square. After they did that, they would mallet a pin and rope on both sides to hold it together. They did this at the top and bottom. They also had a fire pit to cook on and a place to sleep. They did this because they took a raft all the way to Darien. They then would have two people on the raft; one in the bow and one in stern. These rafts could be as long and wide as a football field. That was really big. After this, they would give it to ships at the coast. It would take them about seven days to get there and seven days to get back. Some even stayed because they found better lives.

By the 1900s the rafts changed to steamboats. I learned that they only go twenty-two inches in the water. I thought that was awesome. These are some smart people. I also learned that there was a steamboat race where the boiler exploded! You can still see a part of it on the side of the Altamaha River.

Today you still see all kinds of boats. You see motorboats, speedboats, and pontoon boats. It is interesting to see the boat evolution on the river.

Caleb

Day XIII

Unexpected Layover

Today we woke up and moved out quickly throughout our entire morning routine: packing up campsite, eating, and loading the canoes. The sky has been amazing. There was nothing to obstruct our view, only trees and blue water. Chief Travis and Caleb were together today. Bumblebee was in the bow with his matching yellow life jacket and plastic oar. Chief Travis took a picture of him, and he said it looked like he was in front of a painting. Caleb eagerly showed the rest of the group the first time he had the chance. It really did. The sky has been picturesque all day.

Mitchell and Jaylen were partners today. They struggled but grew within their toil. Neither of them are the most powerful canoeers, so they had to rely more on communicating with one another than sheer strength. Friendly communication is difficult for both, but the two partners improved steadily throughout the day. They improved because they had to, not because they wanted to. Their desire to get downstream without tumping or crashing into the bank overshadowed their reliance on self.

We reached our destination, unbeknownst to the boys, by lunch today. We couldn't go much farther, or we would pass our resupply pick up point for the next day. We ate lunch at the rundown landing and filled up our jerry jugs at an adjacent trailer park. Lunch consisted of string cheese, beef jerky, banana chips, peanuts, and individual fruit cups. We made a game of stuffing all our trash into the sixteen-ounce peanut container.

When we finished lunch, I made it seem like we had a grueling afternoon of paddling in front of us. I talked it up at the meal and had everyone willing but not looking forward to it. I started paddling downstream then veered sharply to the sandbar across from the boat ramp. At first, they didn't know if we were stopping to address an issue, but when they realize we were having another half-day layover, they cheered with excitement.

At the sandbar, we did team jobs after unloading canoes. Afterward, we worked on articles and threw our poles in the water. Will was working on his third article of the trip. He is doing well coming up with new things to write about. Chief Travis left his pole stuck vertically in the sand and went to do something else. All of a sudden, the tension made the pole bend toward the water, but the line broke before he got back to his pole.

I was with the cooks this evening. Mitchell, Will, and I made our original meal plus quesadillas from leftover cheese and pita bread from previous meals. It was an incredibly cheesy dinner. We had so much fun preparing the gourmet meal. They were surprised by the amount of food that was served. We sat in a circle on the sand eating out of our bowls, happy to be on this adventure.

After all the pots, bowls, and spoons needed to prepare and eat the meal were cleaned, the group explored the sandbar. Several old trees were scattered around the huge sandbar, and a few small coves close to our campsite looked like perfect spots to toss a fishing line. A great blue heron fishing for minnows stopped our exploration. The heron had found a pond created when the river receded from flood-stage. Silently we watched it fish as it focused its eyes on a single fish then moved its head back and forth as if it was contemplating its next move. Then it darted its head into the water emerging with a meal it gulped down quickly. Robert found what looked like an old arrowhead on our walk to the other side. And Caleb found what appeared to be several terra cotta pieces. It rained on us for a few minutes then cleared up.

Chief Travis and I prepped for the next day after everyone was settled in their tents. We collaborated on who should be canoe partners, figured out what breakfast and lunch were, and looked at our mileage and noted landmarks to tell the boys to look for when briefing our day at breakfast.

Group Journal: Day 13

Today we woke up and moved out really fast. The reason was we were excited for tomorrow. After we packed up tents, we had breakfast full of cream of wheat and cinnamon apples. After we did that, we loaded canoes and shoved off. Today I was partners with Chief Travis. We canoed a little bit and I looked up at the clouds. I saw a bunch of different shapes in them. Chief Travis took a picture of me, and it looks like I am standing in front of a painting.

Next we came to a boat ramp, took breaks, and we ate lunch. Lunch consisted of string cheese, peanuts, beef jerky, and banana chips. We finished lunch and thought we were going to canoe some more when Chief Jason turned and we went to a sandbar right across from the boat ramp.

After we set up camp we started to finish up some things like articles and letters. We also started fishing. While doing that, I watched Chief Travis's pole and I was about to tell him he had one when it broke the line. He did not like that very much. Tyler caught quite a few fish. We had mac and pepperoni with jello for supper. We then ended our night with a good pow-wow next to the river. I went to bed excited for the next day of the trip.

Caleb

Different Types of Things on the River

There was a group called the Rangers. The Rangers were canoeing the Ocmulgee River. We were canoeing so good that we hit the Altamaha River. When we hit the river, we saw a speed boat practice racing around us so that we could see it. We also went to a museum to see some Indian artifacts and a big old boar. We also saw different types of turtle shells, and a lady also showed us a turtle that she had found in the camping area and it had a messed up shell. Then the Rangers went and explored to go find the huge cypress that was twenty-four steps all the way around and the top was cut off.

Today the Rangers also had a half layover day, but we still had to canoe some miles. When we were canoeing, we had stopped to eat lunch so that we would not be some hungry kids. Then the Rangers canoed across the river so that we could set up camp early because we had a layover day. Next we set up tents and did team jobs for our campsite. When we got done doing team jobs, we did some personal academics so that we could send them back to camp on resupply.

Jaylen

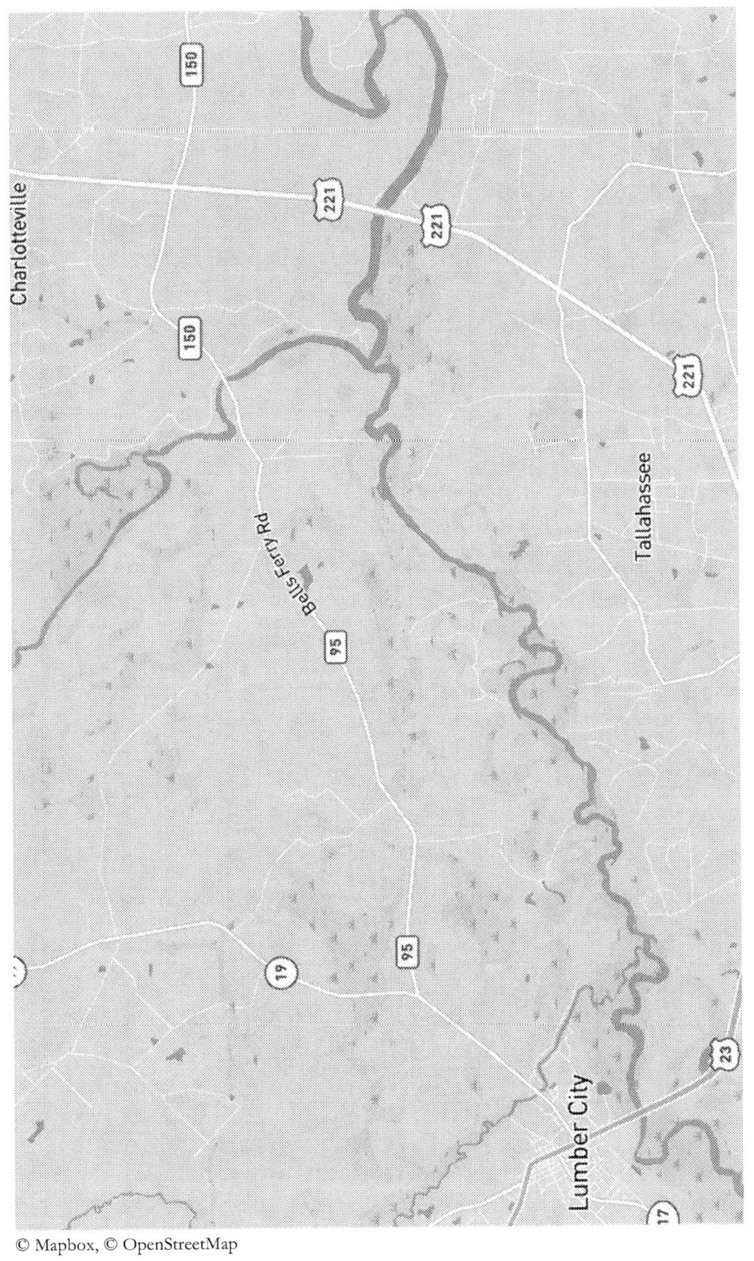
150
Charlotteville
221
221
150
221
Tallahassee
Bells Ferry Rd
95
95
19
23
Lumber City
17

Day XIV

Resupply

There was no redoing our morning routine today for lack of spirit. Everyone got dressed, and their sleeping bags put away in seven minutes and thirty seconds. We took down the tents quickly then split into two groups like usual. One group cooked the meal, and the other started loading the canoes. We canoed about twenty minutes this morning to US Highway 1 for our pick up. We would have gotten there faster, but several canoes got stuck on shallow spots in the middle of the river. The delay helped because we were going to make it to the landing several hours earlier than the van and trailer coming from camp.

Since it did not take long to make our short mileage, we thoroughly cleaned all our gear. We scrubbed dry boxes and life jackets and tarps. We strung a rope to hang the life jackets on and laid the other gear on the ground to dry in the sun. We were in the process of cleaning when Chief Steve, Chief Mike, and Zach showed up. They came an hour early, which turned out to be a blessing.

Chief Mike's absence on the first half of the trip was missed. I was glad to have him back. Zach is our new camper. I can already tell he's going to be fun. He enjoys talking, and I anticipate he will argue when he doesn't get his way and that he'll try to make himself look cool. He seems to be a good-hearted kid. I'm excited to get to know him.

Chief Steve and company brought all our food for the last half of the trip. Chief Steve is our assistant director and director of education at camp. He's six feet tall with a salt and pepper goatee. A bit abrasive at times, he tells it like it is with a genuine passion for the recipient. I try to emulate the structure and discipline he has for himself in my own life. He welcomed us with a smile as he emerged from the green work van. Zach had a nervous smile on his face. He wanted to make a good impression, but I could tell he was nervous. Chief Mike also smiled as he went around giving everyone hugs.

We received new towels, clothes, and other items like soap, duct tape, toilet paper, sunscreen, bug spray, and our much-needed toothpaste. The group organized our food into our empty dry boxes by date. Usually, three days worth of meals can fit into a dry box. Each meal is in its own double-bagged trash bag to prevent water ruining the meal. We had to remember to load them backwards so the later dated ones would be on the bottom. That way we wouldn't have to dig through the dry box each time we needed a meal. The most important items Chief Steve brought with him were letters from home. The boys received mail from their families, and the chiefs got updates from camp.

The group loaded into the van after all our gear was packed and drove to our new put-in point twenty-seven miles up the Oconee River. At first, we did not know where the correct put-in was. We drove to an abandoned road under a bridge with enormous potholes. Chief Steve floored the vehicle so we wouldn't get stuck in the mud. I don't know how we made it through, but we did…twice. We had to turn around to go to the correct landing up the road that actually connected with the river.

Finally, we launched and began the second half of our journey. We were excited to get on the river with our full group. The twelve of us found a campsite around 6:00 p.m. We played a few games with the cloth Frisbee Chief Mike brought while Chief Travis and the cooks prepared the meal. Zach scraped his knee when he fell on a tree stump partially buried in the sand. I doctored him up, and he was right back playing again without one complaint leaving his mouth.

10:04 p.m.

This sandbar has a few mosquitoes and gnats. The moon is incredibly bright. I watched it come up; it looks like a sunrise out here.

Group Journal: Day 14

All right guys, time to get up. We have a big day today. Everyone jumped out of their sleeping bags. Everyone got in a gather-up. Almost everyone got out in seven minutes and thirty seconds. Then we split into two groups. My group, the cooks, made a good meal of oatmeal. Everyone enjoyed the meal. The clean up crew got done washing all the dishes. While everyone was busy, all the canoes got packed and tied down. When everyone was done, we canoed fifteen minutes downstream under a bridge, where Chief Steve will give us resupply.

We cleaned everything including canoes and tents. About an hour after we pulled up Chief Steve pulled up in the van with Chief Mike and a new camper named Zach. Since Zach is new, we got him in the middle of the gather-up and howed him in.

After everyone was done packing the stuff in the trailer, we all got in the van. In the van everyone got a letter. My brother, named Levi, wrote me. After I was done reading my letter, I talked to Chief Steve about my letter and about what we did during the trip.

In the beginning of the road there was a puddle that was deep. Chief Steve looked at it then stepped on the gas pedal. We all went back, but as soon as we hit the water we went forward. When we got out of the van we packed the canoes and got in them. We canoed seven or eight miles to our camp spot. At our camp spot we unloaded the canoes and made camp. We had no gnats or mosquitoes. It was a fun day. I can't wait until tomorrow.

Will

My Day in the Van!

My day at camp was in the camp's van, which was fun. I got to know two chiefs, Chief Steve and Chief Mike. Chief Steve was the driver of the van and Chief Mike and I sat in the seat behind Chief Steve's seat. We took off right after lunch. We hit the road at about 1:30 p.m. and we were on the road until 6:00 p.m. to 7:00 p.m., maybe 7:30 p.m.. On the first day, the night was pretty cool because we stayed in South Carolina at a campsite called Warren Campsite, I think. See the reason why it was so cool was because we got to play a game called horseshoes. The first game I won, the second game Chief Mike won and the last game was won by Chief Steve. At the end it was one for me, one for Chief Mike, and one for Chief Steve. It was an even, friendly game of horseshoes. That is the reason why it was so cool.

In the morning, I learned that the group loves to challenge themselves which I thought was pretty neat. Then we got on the road again. We had to stop at a place to eat. After that was when I finally met the Ranger group.

Zach

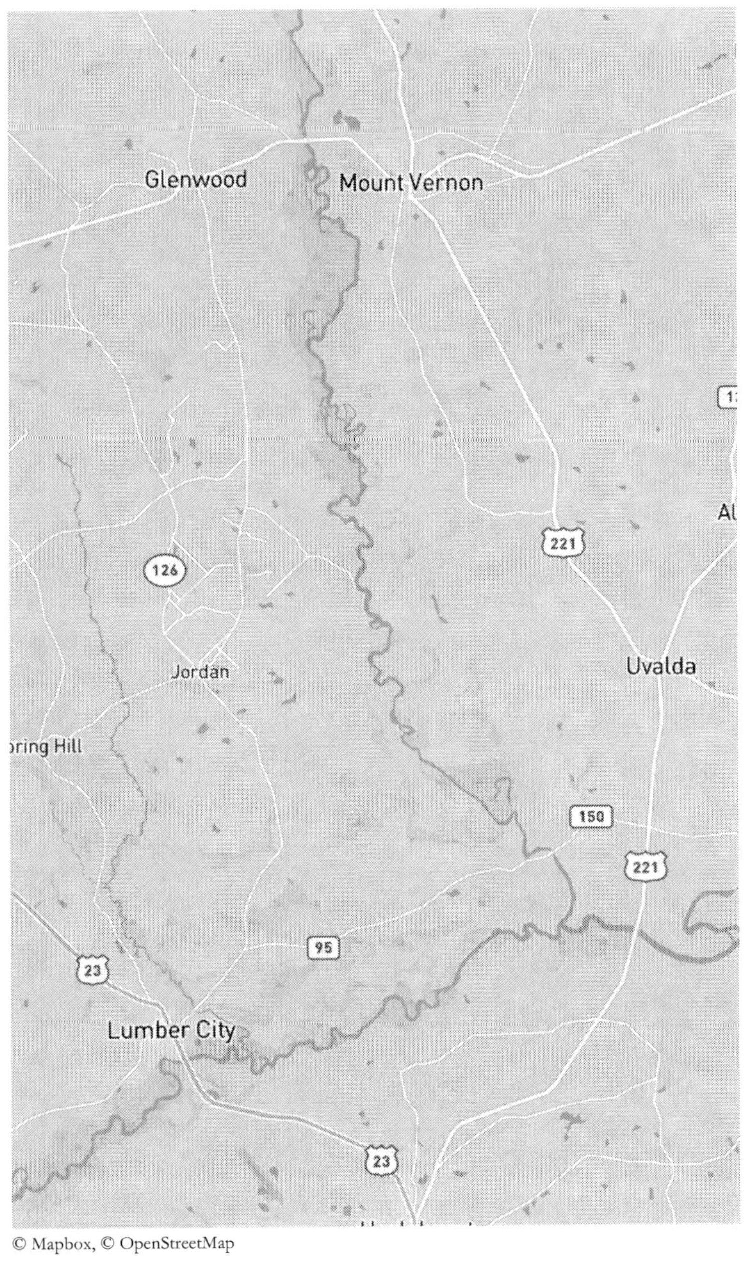

© Mapbox, © OpenStreetMap

Day XV

Blackberry Pie

We canoed twenty miles today before 3:00 p.m. Getting on the river at 8:38 a.m. helped. Zach and Will were in my canoe today. Will was in cargo first. When Chief Steve brought our two other group members, he did not bring an additional canoe for them. I was upset at first because I knew sitting in cargo without the ability to paddle was not a coveted position. I also wanted everyone to say that they paddled the entire trip. There was no way to change it now. I brought up the concern without portraying the burning annoyance going on inside me. Chief Steve said it would be easier for the group to stick together with two campers being in a chief canoe rather than having three canoes with no close supervision. I agreed but was still a little bitter. It would give me opportunities to spend several hours of quality time with just one boy sitting in cargo.

When a boy is in cargo, he sits in the spot directly in front of the stern and may face downstream or turn around and look at the stern. Will faced me today, and we went back and forth asking questions. Will wants to work on computers when he grows up. He also loves drawing and would like to combine the two by incorporating graphic design or website work in his career. Will has drawn the cover page for our camp newspaper several times. He would like to attend a school in Florida to be closer to his cousins. Then, after college, come back to North Carolina to be near his adoptive family.

When that topic fizzled out, I asked both boys, "What do you love?" After a few seconds of silence, I answered with "cheese," "playing basketball," and "traveling" to take the weight off the question. Both told about their favorite restaurants, which got us on the topic of food. I told them of a dream I had the other day about Bolthouse's Green Goodness. I described the sweet, pureed drink I had been craving for the last week.

Zach was in cargo the second half of the day. I asked a bunch of general get-to-know-you questions. He's skinny, athletic, and loves sports. I imagine he's quite good. If we got to our campsite and any food would be waiting for us, it would be pizza. He's observant, often making connections before other boys. He'll know a possible campsite isn't the one we're going to choose because it's too steep or is infested with poison ivy before the others notice. He said one of his favorite things to do it to help people. He enjoys helping his brother the most.

I told him a little of my background and why I chose to come to camp. He told me his parents were never married and also told a story that almost made me cry: Zach was conceived during a one-night stand. His mother found out her husband was cheating on her and went to the bar to drink away her sorrow. At the bar, she met a man who had sex with her. When Zach was a toddler, his father saw him and his mom at a grocery store. It was the first time Zach had seen his father. Zach's dad beat her in the parking lot because she did not get an abortion. I can't fathom the hurt that's gone on in his life. No wonder he said he has difficulty controlling his anger.

We are back at Towns Bluff Landing. We canoed the whole twenty-seven mile stretch of the Oconee in a little over a full day's worth of paddling. This time, we spent the night in the primitive camping zone. Our campsite is between a quarter-mile and a half-mile away from the river nestled in a pine grove, similar to camp. Mr. Bill graciously helped move our gear with the park's truck. I am glad we were able to see him again and tell him thanks for all the insight on the river he gave us a few days ago.

After helping us move, he showed us several arrowheads that were found on the park property. We looked at the ground with excitement, but we didn't find any. While searching for arrowheads, we sought out the monster cypress tree hiding in the forest. This time we found it and realized it really was as big as everyone said it was. The boys used their feet to estimate the circumference and found it to be twenty-seven "feet". The cypress knees coming up from the tree were over seven feet tall and dwarfed all the others in the area. Caleb stood with his back against a massive knee, posing for a picture to get a perspective of how big they were.

During supper preparation, a few of us picked blackberries to put in one of the pie crusts we had for the meal. It was a God thing. God provided for us. Who would have thought the exact day we had a pie crust for a meal we would find a small blackberry patch?

Logan became frustrated when he wasn't chosen to pick berries. He needed to continue helping fix the meal with his partner. The group gathered up, and he took ownership of his selfish action quickly. He is usually the first to volunteer for something fun but becomes timid when we need someone for a challenging task. As a cook, his responsibility was to tend the fire. Mitchell and Robert helped pick berries. While picking, Robert helped Mitchell get unstuck from several briars. Robert is the newest member in the group aside from Zach. If there was any outcast in the group it would be Mitchell, so the initiative Robert showed today was genuine. Robert showed altruism that had no bias, just pure love.

Will had the best breakthrough he has had at camp! He and I were talking about his grandma's funeral. I asked if he would care if his adoptive mom passed away. He said, "Somewhat." We stopped right where we were and talked about it. I was very upset and spoke to him and the group passionately. I couldn't believe he was so apathetic about his mom. I told him about all the effort his mom has put into their relationship, and he has reciprocated nothing in return; no hugs hello or goodbye, no initiation of conversations, nothing.

His view of women has become skewed due to the abuse he incurred during foster care. He brought up that he did not know much of his mom's background from before he was adopted. He said that by filling some of the historical void she could help Will build trust with her. Not knowing as much as he wanted about his adoptive mom caused him to shut down relationally, and his issues of trust and lack of empathy stem from this turmoil.

Will cried for the first time since he's been at camp – a huge breakthrough for him. I pray he is starting to let down the guard he has been building up for so many years. He needs to become vulnerable with others so he can heal. I told him he needed to communicate how he is feeling now to his mom. I suggested he write her a letter tonight but left it totally up to him. Forced change is fake change. After pow-wow, he took the initiative to write his mom a personal letter telling her he loved her and asked about her life before he was adopted. This was in addition to the obligatory letter we ask the boys to write to their families every week. I told him I would mail it when we checked out of the campsite tomorrow.

10:42 p.m.

Since we're staying at a developed landing tonight, everyone was able to take a hot shower. I was able to shave. It was glorious. I feel pampered.

Group Journal: Day 15

Today the Rangers were canoeing the Oconee River because they wanted to have fun. We also had fun with Chief Mike and Zach on the second half of the trip. We also had fun because today we got to come thank and see Mr. Bill. Mr. Bill is the guy who showed us the Indian artifacts and a big cypress tree. When we saw the big cypress, tree everybody was surprised because it was twenty-four feet all the way around.

Today we also had fun because we were given a nice campsite from Mr. Bill. Our day also was fun because we took showers and put on new clothes because we did not want to smell bad anymore. We wanted to smell good. I also had fun because we hit the Altamaha in only two days because we were beasting on our miles. Last night, we had an awesome meal and it was Will's favorite meal, cowboy stew. We also had fun yesterday because we solved a problem with Logan and Will. I also learned that you should love your parents no matter what. We also went rambling, and I found some cypress knees. The biggest that we found was for Chief Mike. We also had a good lunch because we had deserved to eat lunch because we did so good on our miles.

If you ever hear of this article, always remember who it is from because it might mean something to me and you. I love my group, the Rangers because they support me a lot.

Jaylen

Day XVI

Long-nosed Gar

Mr. George, another employee of Towns Bluff Landing and a chain smoker, helped bring all our gear back to the landing this morning with his truck. Will and I rode with Mr. George. The rest hiked the trail to the landing. We made it a race to see if we could get everything unloaded and down to the water before the group arrived. Will and I unloaded the truck and got all but one of the canoes in the water before the group showed up. He can be motivated by others, but has a more difficult time motivating himself.

We moved in unison, picking up the dry boxes by the handles and ran to the water's edge. He asked, "Think you can beat me back to the truck, Chief?" with a smirk and began running before I could answer. He's short, but strong. The heaviest of gear gave him no trouble. The remaining dry boxes and other gear were left for the others on the sidewalk a few feet from the bed of the truck. Will can do so much when he puts his mind to it. I wish he would do that more often, especially without prompting.

On the way to join us at the boat dock, Mitchell lost his glasses. He didn't notice he lost them until he was at the dock with no clue as to where they could be down the trail. I had already left to talk with Ms. Anna, the manager of the landing and to mail Will's letter. The group set off without me in search for Mitchell's glasses. Ms. Anna wants to write an article for the newspaper that features the group. It will give us publicity and also highlight Towns Bluff Landing. Zach found Mitchell's glasses on the dirt road near the cliff overlooking the river. It was right where Mr. Bill told us several people found arrowheads while post-hole digging to put in a fence. His glasses were better than an arrowhead at that moment. Zach was hailed as a hero.

We shoved off and paddled downstream. The ride was fun, but seemed to be going slowly. Caleb was at my bow with Tyler in cargo. They switched after lunch. Logan and Jaylen nearly tumped the canoe when they hit a log. Their canoe ran up on the log stopping their forward motion and began spinning them. When they were perpendicular to the river, the current began to tip the boat. Jaylen leaned upstream to compensate for the boat leading to one side. Logan had his paddle in the water frantically trying to get free from the log.

Chief Mike and Zach hurried upstream to help them get off the log. They eventually got off but had taken on a lot of water in the process. The submerged log made a small crack in the bottom of their boat. I don't think it will be too much of a problem. If it becomes an issue, we can duct tape the inside and outside of the canoe. They had to pull off as soon as they were free and untie everything to make their canoe light enough to flip upside-down to remove the water. With that much water in the canoe, it would sit too low risking an all-out tump, not to mention it would be difficult to gain momentum down the river. Our dry boxes do not live up to their name. Everything in the boxes was soaked.

I helped Zach write a journal entry this evening after supper. His writing skills are not where they should be, so we'll be giving as much help as we can without doing it for him. Even though we'll do the bulk of the written work, Zach will be able to take full ownership of the entry because it'll be his words. The group helped Zach come up with three goals over our meal. All of the guys came up with their own goals for the trip. Since Zach came late, we helped him come up with some for the last half of our journey. They are:

- I will get to know other people's stories.
- I will respect chiefs and the group by listening to them.
- I will learn more about trees and animals by writing two articles about them.

Tyler caught a long-nosed gar tonight, his first. He used a chunk of fish someone caught earlier. At first, the gar took the bait, but spit it out once Tyler began reeling in. This happened over and over. Finally, Tyler loosened the drag and let the fish swim away with the bait until he was sure the fish swallowed it. When he set the hook and tightened the drag, the pole bent toward the water. Tyler's eyes squinted as if focused on something with all his might. A little worried about breaking the line, he tired the fish out, letting it swim around then reeling in a little.

Everyone was excited for him when he brought it to shore. The boys all gathered around to look at the monster. It snapped and flopped around a few times, but he eventually gained control. As Tyler held it, the rest of us admired the two and a half foot gar. It was a cream-white color peppered with black scales. Tyler released it, with a victorious smile.

God closed our day with another beautiful sunset. There isn't much to do tonight to prepare for the morning, so I plan on catching up on reading.

9:15 p.m.

Group Journal: Day 16

Today was very interesting because we canoed down the river and went to a museum in Towns Bluff. Mitchell had lost his glasses and I found a Timber Wolf knife at the campground. It was pretty cool. And then we found Mitchell's glasses on the trail! So when we got back we all went inside the museum and looked around. I took my picture with a big black boar. We also saw Indian arrowheads and turtle shells. A man helped us out with loading our dry boxes and other supplies up to the campground and back.

This just in, Tyler just caught a long-nosed gar!

Back to the day. Oh, then we met this real nice woman named Anna, who is going to write in a newspaper about us and our trip that we are doing on the river. We took off. I was with Chief Mike which is always fun to me. We talked about my family and how they are all sick and have cancer which made me tear up just a little bit, but I am fine now. I personally think he really understood what I was saying to him.

Oh, guess what? Chief Mike and I helped Logan and Jaylen from tumping over and we turned around to help them. We pushed them around and we ended up turning instead of them so I had to climb on top of a dry box and got them out of trouble of tumping over. And then we found a campsite, then went fishing and we ate, then went to bed. The end.

Zach

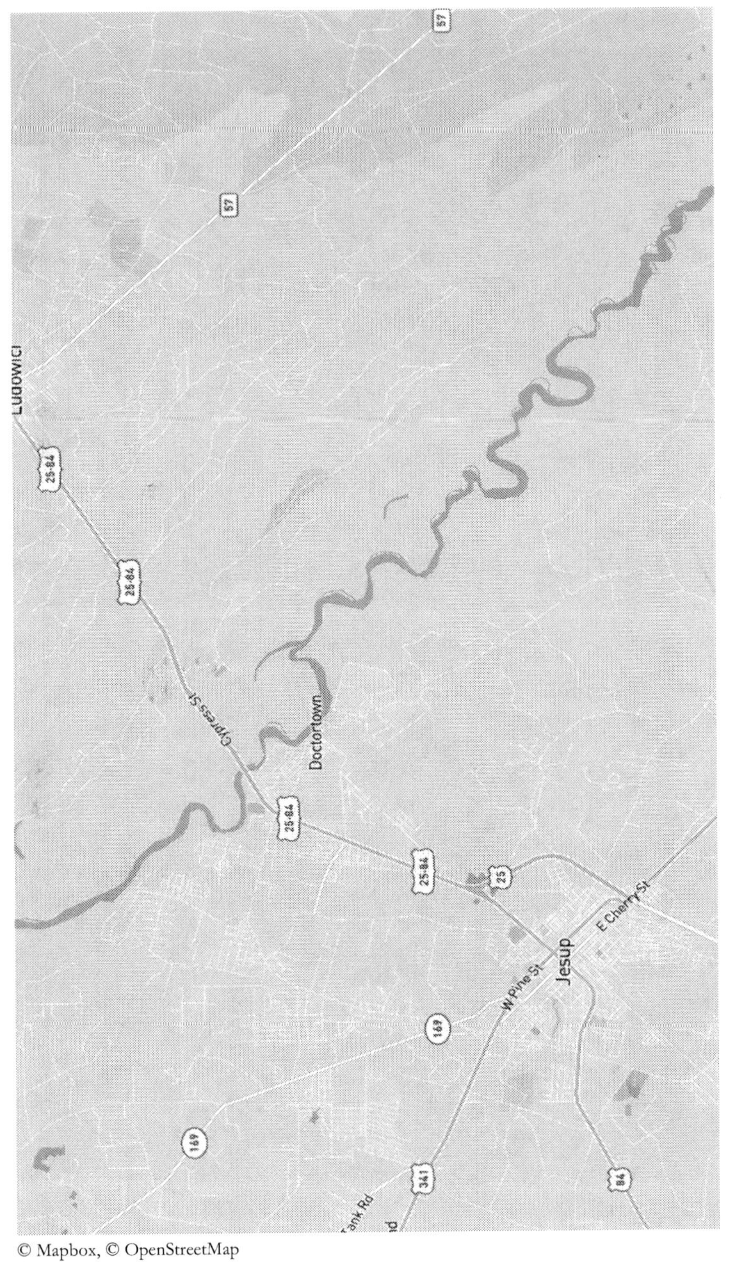

© Mapbox, © OpenStreetMap

Day XVII

Leftovers

Logan and I were together all day today. We talked about old forts we had built when we were younger, family, and his desire to go home. Almost every boy at camp has a longing to be back with his family. This desire is healthy when used to complete their purpose at camp, namely their goals, and return to a more unified and structured family system. An unhealthy desire hinders the boys' progress at camp. Their minds dwell on home, and they will neglect working on what they came to camp to work on. Some will spitefully not work on their goals because their parents refuse to take them out of the program. They do this until they realize their parents really mean what they say. Others will try to cause enough chaos to be kicked out of camp, but it rarely works. Causing chaos only prolongs their time at camp because they aren't working on their goals.

Though I love them, I don't want any of the boys to be at camp. They should not be here, away from their families, in the first place. Less than ideal circumstances and the responses from themselves and the people around them have caused problems that need to be addressed. Camp addresses those issues and prepares the boys to be home with their families as soon as they're ready. Logan is no exception. He's been here ten months. A habitual liar, Logan has sought to be accepted. He's smoked weed, fabricated elaborate tales of overseas travels, and degraded others in attempts to fit in with the cool crowd. At camp, he's slowly becoming comfortable with himself and is continuing to wrestle with the fact that his birth mom wants nothing to do with him.

During our conversation about family, we began talking about prayer. Trips are such an awesome opportunity to have conversations with the boys on a whole other level. Canoe partners share the same canoe for five hours without many distractions. And we can't really go anywhere without the other person in the canoe. All the superficial conversations run out after a while, and we have to start talking about things of substance.

I have been encouraging the boys to tell each other their stories. Boys come into camp at different times and may not know why certain people are there or may not know a person's background as well as another camper who has been around longer. The more a person tells a story, the more they accept it, own it, and—in these boys' cases—can overcome the setbacks. This conquering of one's past can only happen through love and encouragement. Both are key components of camp.

We had long stretches of boring, unbending river. In the afternoon, Logan and I stopped at a landing to figure out our exact location on the river. We met two fishermen who were wrapping up for the day. They just put their boat on the trailer when we walked up. They told us we were at the Carter's Bight Landing and spoiled us with leftover food and drinks. Vienna sausages (Chad's favorite), bottled water, PowerAde, crackers, chips, Nutterbutter bars, and mini Oreos were in the bag they gave. We greatly appreciated the gifts and went back to the group. The others pulled off a little downstream of us and couldn't see the white plastic bag we carried our snacks in. I told Logan not to let the others know what the fishermen had given us.

A minute or two later, we caught up with the group, and they shoved their canoes back into the water. Logan smiled inconspicuously as we canoed with the plastic bag under my seat. Then we passed under 169 Highway where we stopped again. Since I did not have any cell phone service at the landing, I thought I would try my luck at the bridge. It paid off. I had a few service bars.

I called the paper plant in Jesup to see if someone could give us a tour that afternoon or tomorrow. I was rudely informed that it was not a paper plant but a pulp facility, with a strong emphasis on the first p in pulp. People on the river and chiefs at camp who have been on the river before had always referred to it as a paper plant. The curt public relations lady was not going to help us take a tour of the plant. She said she was the only one able to coordinate tours and would not refer me to any other employee. I guess it's not incredibly important that we take a tour anyway.

While I was making the call, the group opened the bag of snacks the two fishermen gave. They told me Chad's eyes lit up when he saw the Vienna sausages. The rest of the group gladly let him have those. They figured there would be more sweet snacks for themselves. They played with the cloth Frisbee until I returned. Then we tried to make a few more miles before stopping for the day.

At our riverside home this evening, Robert and I read through the Sermon on the Mount[5] while the others were fishing. I think Robert seemed genuinely interested. I'm not sure he has gotten much exposure to Jesus. Mitchell talked about the Book of James over lunch. One of Mitchell's goals is to read James and talk to the group about it. I'm glad he is sticking with it even if he doesn't want to. The group has been holding him accountable. He seems to appreciate it afterward. Sometimes I think Mitchell is intimidated by success; he feels like it's unobtainable for him because it hasn't happened often in his life. Almost all of the boys have that struggle. Sometimes he doesn't want to read or talk about what he read, but when the group holds him to it, he is thankful for the accountability. I enjoy incorporating Jesus, God, and the Bible into conversations.

After a few helpings of enchilada pie and forty-five minutes of fishing, I read to the group the story of Daniel's vision[6] where he prays and waits for three weeks for an answer. We talked about how God answers prayer. God's answer may be "yes," "no," or "wait." God's answer may not be fulfilled in the way we thought it would. Several of the boys spoke up, telling their own stories of prayer.

Along with their stories, the boys also gave advice to each other. I just sat back, listened, and supported what they were saying. Some of the guys have similar family situations and have dealt with the same issues. The boys who have gone through difficult times encouraged the others to keep moving forward, that there was light at the end of the tunnel. Encouragement means so much more when it's given by a peer who's been through the same thing.

The mosquitoes let out their fury after pow-wow. I went straight into the tent, thinking that I could do all the prep work for tomorrow morning inside. I brought in our trip folder. Flipping through the pages, I looked over the maps and figured out what we're having for breakfast tomorrow. My reading goal is complete. I finished the Gospel of Luke today and will be continuing in the Old Testament with Ruth.

9:12 p.m.

Group Journal: Day 17

Today we woke up to the sound of chiefs' voices saying, "Wake up." Then we had breakfast of Cap'n Crunch, Mini Wheats, and Frosted Flakes with an orange drink. After breakfast and cleaning up, we scanned out and then we got canoe partners and headed out. My canoe partner was Robert and we did another bit of talking and singing. We talked about guitars for a while and then we talked about music. It eventually got us to singing some music, and then we were canoeing and singing more and more.

Then we stopped for a lunch of Mini Wheats, dried pineapple, pepperoni and dried apples with Ritz crackers. When we got to the end of our wonderful afternoon meal we switched canoe partners. Then we got in our canoes according to our new seats in the canoes and headed out a little further.

When we got to a boat ramp some people told us that we were close to the bridge that we were looking for. We stopped at a sandbar a little bit after the bridge and we ate a snack that some fishermen gave us. It was water, PowerAde, Lance crackers, Nutterbutters, and mini Oreos. Plus the most amazing snack in the world, Vienna Sausages. Then we got back in the canoes and headed for a campsite. In the canoe as cargo for Chief Mike and Mitchell, I talked about homesday, and we talked about some of the good I can do for my mom and dad over homesday. We also talked about how to make good friends.

While fishing, the cooks made an amazing meal of enchilada pie. It was an amazing meal and we very thoroughly enjoyed it. Then we headed to pow-wow and then to bed. Our spirit was very good today, and I hope that tomorrow is the same.

Chad

Day XVIII

Unsweet Applesauce

This morning the chiefs assigned Chad and Tyler to the same canoe. Tyler is one of the best canoeers in the group. One of his weaknesses is trying to do everything himself. This isn't limited to just canoeing. He won't tell anyone what is bothering him. He won't ask for help if he doesn't know how to spell a word or tie a specific knot. This usually results in him failing at a task or not being able to handle his emotions and ultimately taking them out in terrible ways. When he's frustrated at someone, he'll stay silently angry for so long that he'll end up sabotaging whomever he's angry with.

We decided to have Tyler in bow and Chad in stern. Chad struggles with steering. He overcorrects his strokes and ends up zigzagging all over the river. Our goal today was to have Tyler teach Chad rather than try to correct Chad's sterning himself. For far this trip, Tyler will seize the helm by ruddering from the bow before trusting his partner or putting in the effort to teach.

At first, Tyler tried to control the canoe from the front. He could do it, but I stressed the importance of teaching Chad, canoeing with Chad rather than for him. He understood, but still didn't want to go back and forth downstream.

Even with Tyler's help, Chad had a difficult time keeping the nose of the canoe pointed downstream. If Chad doesn't understand something, he'll either fabricate something, pretending it's right, or quit. This time he couldn't pretend he was going straight. He resorted to complaining, seeking to justify it really wasn't his fault before putting down his paddle. But he couldn't really quit either. It was the perfect growth opportunity. Both Chad and Tyler improved throughout the day. They began to work cohesively and used one another's strengths.

Today was a long day. We got on the river before 9:00 a.m. and paddled fifteen miles before resting for lunch. It was another trail mix day, so we stayed in the canoes and passed out individual bags. We were able to get a few more miles this way. In addition to trail mix, we each received a cup of applesauce. We had to slurp it out of the container because we didn't want to unpack spoons from the dry box. A few of the boys used their thin aluminum wrappers creatively and bent them into makeshift spoons they could scoop the applesauce with.

Caleb had a bad attitude because he didn't get sweetened applesauce. When he complained about not getting his desired fruit cup we made it a serious issue. Little things like this happen fairly regularly with Caleb, but there's a bigger issue underneath that often goes unaddressed. At home, he manipulates his mom to spend money they don't have taking him out to eat or on other unnecessaries just because he wants them. The single parent of five children, she doesn't have enough money for trivial disposables like video games or constant fast food. Sometimes he's blinded to his own selfishness, but this afternoon we wanted to make it blatantly obvious that complaining over trivial things like sugary applesauce ends up hurting the people he loves most. We told him he didn't have to eat it. We compared this incident to what happens at home. His selfishness was causing his family to suffer. I held my hand out to receive it offered to take it back. I asked what he was going to do. "Are you going to give it back and not eat or are you going to take what you get and be thankful for it? Getting the sweetened kind is not an option." He kept it and ate the meal in silence.

My canoe partners were Mitchell and Will. Mitchell read a little of First Samuel to me while in cargo. Will helped create a warehouse list for our backpack trip. We wanted to take a backpack trip when we returned to camp and were trying to get a jumpstart planning it. While he sat in the middle of the canoe, he jotted down ideas of what to bring on the backpack trip in the spiral notebook I brought along. All three of us brainstormed together, and also asked the other canoes for their input. The group already has ideas for six days' worth of meals planned for our next adventure.

We canoed over twenty miles to Jesup, where we were met with tons of weekenders camping on the sandbars. Passing Jaycee's Landing, we set up camp close to the highway. This was the only vacant spot we could find. Chief Travis went back to Jaycee's Landing to get water with Mitchell and Will. They loaded all the jerry jugs into one canoe and paddled upstream. They returned with our much-needed water and also brought a twenty-four pack of Pepsi a generous Samaritan gave them. I had a swig of the drink, and felt like it was instantly dissolving my teeth. It was the first time I had anything but water on the trip and the first time for a carbonated beverage in four or five months.

A lady at the landing who ran the bait shop and store gave us some toothpaste. We've been running low and having to use Dr. Bronner's castile soap that doubles as toothpaste. She obtained the toothpaste by gathering anything she could spare from her home. We received a few half-empty tubes and a Dora the Explorer themed one. We were so thankful for her willingness to help us.

Out of nowhere, I asked if one of the boys was willing to give the rest of their Pepsi to someone else. Caleb was the first one to speak up and donate the remainder of his. I couldn't believe what I just heard! I was shocked because we had seen how selfish he was with the applesauce earlier this afternoon. He must have had a change of heart. I had intended on seeing who was the first to be selfless, then reward them with the Pepsi I wasn't going to drink. We paused our group conversation to focus on Caleb's selfless act. I asked the other boys to put words on Caleb's progress and tell him how they had seen him grow throughout the trip. I gave him the remainder of my drink and told him that if he'd let his group look after him, rather than him fighting to fulfill his own desires, all his needs and even some of his wants will be taken care of.

During our evening activity of fishing, I talked with Zach about his family life. By the way he said, "Yes sir" so quickly after everything or "Sorry" every time he made a mistake, I could tell he was probably abused. Even his mannerisms spoke volumes. He quickly went out of his way to get on my good side. He's very observant and watches the chiefs to see if we look frustrated or angry. If Zach suspects anything uncomfortable between him and another person, he'll do his best to avoid the situation. While we were talking, he shared that the uncle who lives with him hits him and that his dad has laid a hand on him before too.

We didn't catch anything. A few of the boys had more fun trying to catch minnows in a small cove. Beneath one of the rocks lay a water snake. Tyler saw it and was able to catch it. It was less than a foot long and mad it had been caught. Tyler let Mitchell hold it. Mitchell is a lot more nervous around snakes than Tyler, especially since one scared him so bad when it fell in the canoe earlier in the trip. He's never really handled one before. Mitchell ended up squeezing it too tight, and the snake bit him. The scare was worse than the pain.

Receiving a snakebite instantly elevated Mitchell to rock star status in the group. Logan wanted a share of the popularity and asked Tyler to let the snake bite him. All the commotion caused me to go over to see what was going on. When I found out I was livid. What if Tyler misidentified the snake? I have no idea why they wanted to get bit; I guess boys will do foolish things.

Tyler had a rough day with listening to his group but kept trying to overcome the difficulty. These issues were relatively minor: not paying attention to his canoe partner, selective listening when chiefs asked him to do something, and not thinking about what people are really asking him to do. His battle with hedonism is a tough one. Unaddressed, these issues can spiral downhill quickly.

Robert got caught lying earlier today. We discussed it, and he got right with everyone. I wanted to address the issue quickly and with moderate severity since Robert is so new. We didn't need to dwell on it, but I wanted to let him know where the group stands with lying.

Caleb talked with me after pow-wow about thoughts that stemmed from this afternoon's issue about the applesauce. He was torn up about his decision on what to do after he leaves camp: either staying at home to help take care of and provide for his family or escaping to find an alternative place to live because home-life is just too hard. It's not his decision to make; he needs to follow his mom's guidance, but that's not something a kid should even think about. I feel so bad for these guys' situations.

9:41 p.m.

By the end of the day, Chad was a better sterner.

I can see the pulp plant from our campsite. I can hear it along with the faint murmur of traffic.

Group Journal: Day 18

Today we woke up with good spirits and we got on the river before nine o'clock. Before lunch we paddled fifteen miles. My partner was Chad. I was his bow. He is getting good at stern if he stays focused. Since we had trail mix for lunch, we decided to float down the river and eat. It is Saturday and there were a lot of boats coming out to fish or just play around.

After lunch, we paddled about ten miles to a bridge. Since we needed water we stayed across the bridge and a group went up to a landing to get the water. Will, Mitchell, and Chief Travis went to get the water, and a nice man that worked at the store bought the group a twenty-four pack of Pepsi. We fished while the group got water. We never did catch one but I did find a water snake. The snake was about a foot long. I tried to let Mitchell hold the snake but Mitchell squeezed it and it bit him and Logan. We talked to the group about how to hold a snake. Maybe they learned how to hold the snakes without being bit. The rest of the night went peaceful.

Tyler

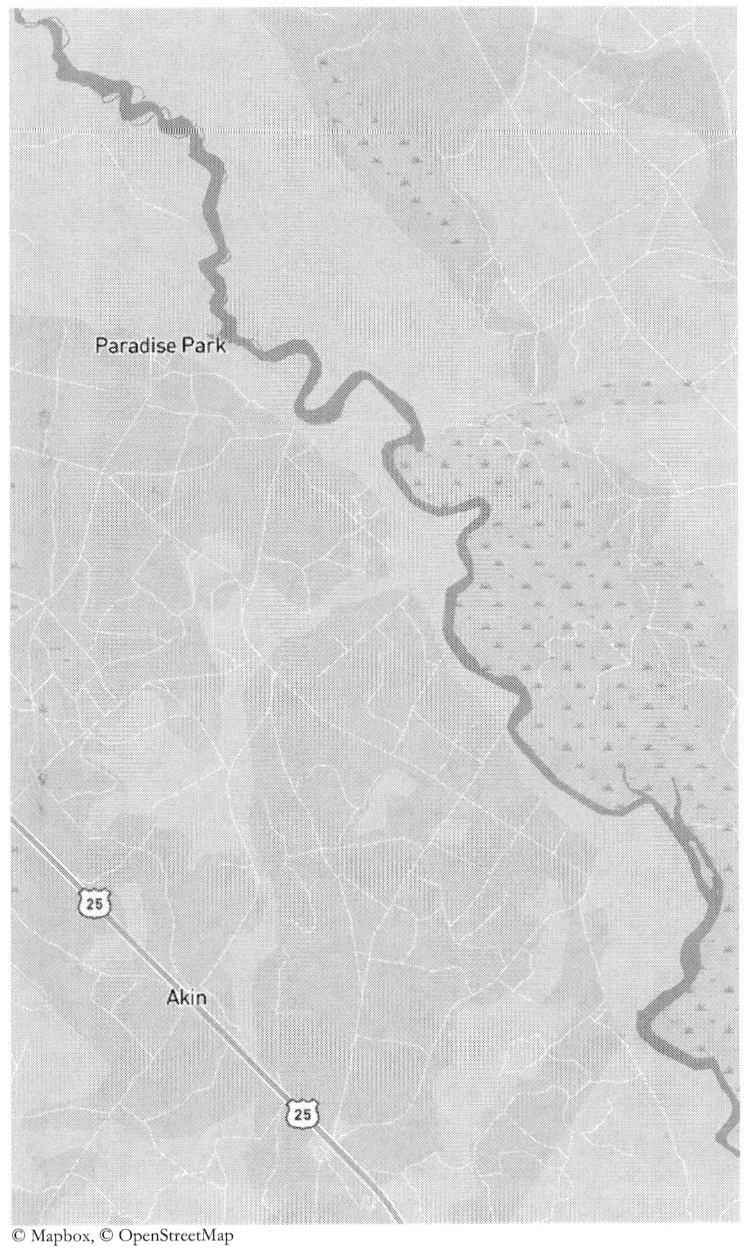
Paradise Park
25
Akin
25

Day XIX

Bloated Beast

We left Jesup this morning in search of the great unknown. Past the pulp facility, the water turned an ink blue color and had an unfamiliar stench. Shortly after the water color changed, we saw the remnants of an old paddleboat. It was barely distinguishable; partially submerged and plated with rust. From there, sandbars became less frequent, and the terrain dropped, leaving a swampy feel to the area. Usually, we see sandbars around nearly every turn. Now we went over an hour between bars.

Several alligators were spotted. One of the boys saw a dead one near the bank on the left side under some low lying trees. The group thought it was interesting, but we couldn't all get around it at the same time. Chief Mike tied the gator to a rear painter so we could get a closer look after lunch. It had gone into full rigor mortis and stunk far worse than the boar we found on the second day. While dragging it down the river, Chief Mike popped the bloated beast. The boys reeled as their nostrils were set on fire. Fifty feet away, I could smell when it popped. There was no way I was going to get near it until I absolutely had to.

When we found a sandbar to eat lunch, we sat far away from the gator and its smell. Chief Mike's canoe brought it ashore. After lunch, we investigated and found it was close to five feet long and had no signs of traumatic death. The boys noticed webbed feet and that several of its teeth were already missing. We didn't linger around longer than we had to and pressed on down the river.

Sandbars began reappearing after lunch. It was a lot less stressful for me to start seeing them again. Temperatures were high today. Everyone could see the haze coming up from the river; we could actually see the water evaporating. The boys noticed it and I had them try to figure out what it was. They said smoke, but I asked them to smell. When they couldn't smell smoke, they guessed mist. I told them to keep going. Where was the mist coming from? They eventually discovered the haze was water evaporating from the river.

We pulled over our canoes shortly before 3:00 p.m., set up camp, did team jobs, then changed into swimwear. A few of the locals upstream said the temperature would get cooler the farther downstream we went. As of yet, I haven't been able to call their claims true. It was another hot one today. We swam for a while then got the camp suds out and bathed, but not before playing a few games of Stealth. When we got out of the water, we retrieved the duffle bag with a clean set of roll-ups. It felt so good to get out of our three-day-old clothes. My socks were starting to become stiff. We put the old roll-ups in the bag and marked them as dirty.

For our meal, we ate Ramen spiced with Texas Pete hot sauce and syrup we had leftover from a previous meal. I think boned chicken is the best all-around meat we can take on a canoe trip. It's not as salty as the other packable meats and

Chicken and Ramen

Summer Sausage
Canned Chicken
Ramen Noodles
Flour Tortillas
Canned Mandarin Oranges
Canned Lima Beans
Texas Pete

tastes great with pasta. We had plenty of leftovers after we served seconds, so we asked questions to divvy out the remainder of the pot.

Usually, the chiefs will ask questions concerning trip knowledge like "How many miles have we canoed so far?" "How do you spell Ocmulgee?" or "What types of trees did the raftmen build their rafts out of?" Occasionally we'll ask if anyone knows another person's goals. It's important that the other boys know them. Knowing what goals everyone is working on provides motivation and more accountability for others to work on their own. When we exhausted all of those questions, the chiefs asked personal trivia questions, so the boys will know our backgrounds better. I asked them if they knew Chief Mike's high school mascot and my basketball jersey number. I asked if they knew my sister's name and what Chief Travis's college degree was in.

Caleb had a rough night with the questions tonight. He would either not know the right answer when we called on him or would know the answer, but we called on someone else before him. His expressions were hilarious when he knew something but wasn't called on. As soon as the question was asked, his hand would dart in the air and wave back and forth like an elementary school kid who wants to get the teacher's attention. When I asked the questions, I usually wouldn't call on him first if his hand was waving like that. He took it well and laughed it off. I commended his enthusiasm but tried to get him to show it more maturely. Maturity is one of the things I want him to go back to school and have more of. At sixteen, he is more concerned with Pokémon than getting his driver's license.

After our spiced ramen supper, we devised a plan for our evening of fishing and academic work. Everyone but me drank the remaining Pepsi Mr. Larry purchased for us the other day. During that time, I read more in the *Hunger Games* series. Robert and Mitchell interrupted me to sing me a rap they just wrote. I was honored to be their audience and would gladly be interrupted again. The feeling I get when boys are eager to show me something will never get old. That was the highlight of my day.

9:27 p.m.

Group Journal: Day 19

Today we docked out of Jesup. Before we did that though, we loaded canoes and ate a breakfast of grits and bacon bits. We loaded canoes and I was with Chief Jason in the Dawn Tredder (the XL). We talked about my feelings and what I felt about my home situation. We sang a little bit and we also noticed that the water turned an awful color. After a while, we came across a dead alligator. It was a medium-sized one. We came up with some questions about it. We also guessed that it had been dead for about a week or two. We left it on a sandbar after we ate lunch.

We continued on our way and found a sandbar about half an hour after lunch. We camped, and I don't think I have said how HOT it is. It feels like I am slow roasting in an eighteen quart roaster on high. It is horrible. They said it will be cooler as we go down but I have yet to feel it.

After we made campsite, we did team jobs. We went swimming. Swimming was fun because we played Stealth. We swam and we took showers. It felt amazing to get my body washed. I also washed my swimming shirt. Next we started to cook supper and started to fish. When we went fishing we found a dead turtle. We ate supper full of Ramen. I felt I was on jeopardy more than I was in a meal. It was because chiefs asked a lot of questions for extra food. When I was done I had negative 500 points. I need to ask more questions about chiefs. After we ate, we went fishing and drank some Pepsi. It was cool.

Caleb

The Way the Group is Changing

Trips are very, very good for a group because things get tough. For instance, if a guy in the group has been getting seconds on food a lot and he sees a guy that has been dropping out for other people so that they can eat, the guy that has been getting seconds might give his food to the other person so that they can eat.

At the beginning of the trip, our group was slacking on supporting, responding, and meeting our time goals. Now our group has been doing a lot better at supporting and responding. We still need to work on our time goals a little bit, but we have been growing a lot as a whole.

Robert was a new camper at the beginning of the session, and he is jumping right into our group. He is starting to call people out in their problems and supporting chiefs at all times. Zach is trying to follow people and doing what is right. He is really paddling hard and doing his goal which is learning other people's stories. This river trip is helping the Rangers become stronger in spiritual, mental, and physical aspects.

Tyler

Day XX

Too Much Pepsi

This morning, Will asked to talk with me one-on-one. He told me someone toughed him in the tent last night. Instantly, our conversation made me nervous, and I asked for more details. Last night Zach waved his hand in front of Will's face and brushed his eyebrow. Thank goodness it wasn't something else. We gathered the group up. Cooks paused making breakfast and we walked out of our camping area and sat down.

We asked if anything had gone on in the tents last night. We gave everyone an opportunity to get straight with the group. Some kept their mouths shut for a while, but we wouldn't let it go. We sat for over an hour, making sure everyone talked everything out that they needed to, and all the boys felt like every situation was dealt with and resolved. We made sure Will felt at peace with the situation and that he would be kept safe. Caleb and Chad admitted they were giggling in their tent last night too. The last thing I want to have in the group is a bunch of secrets or something sexual going on between the boys.

I blame the unsettledness on the Pepsi, not ill intent. We drank the soda after our meal, and the boys weren't used to caffeine. I'm sure they were awake longer than they normally would. I was upset at myself for not checking when I suspected something going on last night. That was bad chiefing on my part. I'm extremely relieved it wasn't more serious. That will not happen again.

We saw just as many alligators today as we did yesterday. One let Will and me get really close. It was blazing hot today. We didn't leave campsite until 10:30 a.m. due to discussing the issues that went on last night. An hour later, we stopped to refill Nalgenes. On the river we sang songs and wrote songs for our skit at the end of the session that we will present to the other two groups.

At the end of every six-week session, each group performs a skit to convey to an audience of camp supporters what they did and what they learned during that time. One idea we've been throwing around is doing a musical with all the songs we've sung downstream. Chief Travis and Chad have remixed *Country Roads* by John Denver. Some of the boys and I have rewritten *Old Texas* as *Old Georgia.* And Caleb's been singing plenty of songs for our musical.

Everyone drained their Nalgene again by 1:30 p.m. At that time we found a campsite a little downstream from Williamsburg Landing, twenty-six miles from Darien. It was a big sandbar on the left side of the river. We moved all our stuff across the sand, close to the tree line.

When our late lunch was over, we set up tents then went swimming to escape from the heat. Following swimming, we explored the woods behind our campsite. We identified some of the trees we had looked up earlier on the trip. All of us flipped logs to see what kind of bugs we could turn up. We found crickets and worms that the boys held on to for fish bait. Some of the guys caught and played with large red and black millipedes called American giant millipedes.

We began our duo of fishing and academics after our exploration while cooks prepared the meal. The days are winding down to our celebration. As I was eating, my mind wandered back to the book I am reading. I thought of Katniss and of how I will admire the food at the celebration like she did at the Capitol.

I'm tired. I love being physically spent at the end of the day. We had a lot of fun swimming this afternoon. Some of the boys wanted to test my strength by seeing if they could dunk me. I wanted to have fun and play around, but I also didn't want to have the boys try to show everyone that they are stronger than a chief. If I ever have to restrain one of them for being violent toward themselves or someone else, I don't want them to have a false confidence that I couldn't handle the situation just because they could push my head underwater. They were unsuccessful in dunking me. My watch stopped working again while we were swimming then magically came back to life while the cooks were cleaning. I'm thankful it started working. I go off my watch to see when we need to start looking for a campsite rather than the sun.

One of my goals tomorrow will be to go above and beyond with enthusiasm. I want to see how much it helps lift the boys' spirits and creates momentum.

Group Journal: Day 20

Today we woke up after a hot night. It was 89 degrees when we went to bed at around 9:00 p.m.. We had some guys playing around in tents last night, so we had some good problem solving as a group. This took at least an hour, but we all can take a lot from it. We can learn to speak up for what we know is right. We can learn to help out even when we feel ashamed or guilty. After that learning session, Logan, Chad, Mitchell, and I worked on making breakfast. We mixed up pancake mix, water, powdered milk, Coca-Cola, blueberries, and peanut butter to make the best scrambled pancakes this side of the Altamaha. We had to continually mix the pancakes so they wouldn't burn. We even put the mix into two pots to help it thicken quicker. It was really good and we had leftovers. It took a while to clean up, so the rest of the group played Ultimate Frisbee.

We got on the river after 10:00 a.m. and continued until a late lunch. That morning we saw more alligators that were small in size. We, as a group, sang songs, wrote songs for our skit, and learned more about each other by sharing stories. We stopped at Williamsburg Landing, which was about twelve miles from where we started. We ended up setting up camp across river on a big beach behind an island. We ate lunch and set up camp. The river was very sandy and shallow where we were at, so we went for a swim. It was very relaxing and cooling on this upper ninety-degree day. We also had great woods we wanted to explore so we went and found some very different insects. Some of them looked good to use for fish bait. We flipped a lot of logs and tore open many dead trees to find these critters. With all that we collected, we needed to look them up in the Audubon book and, of course, use them as bait.

So the cooks got to work, and the rest of us worked on academics and went fishing. Mitchell was working really hard on an article, Tyler was working really hard on fishing, Will was working really hard on math, and we were all having fun. Three small fish were caught right away. Then some big ones got away. It has been a good day of problems and guys talking out because of them.

Chief Mike

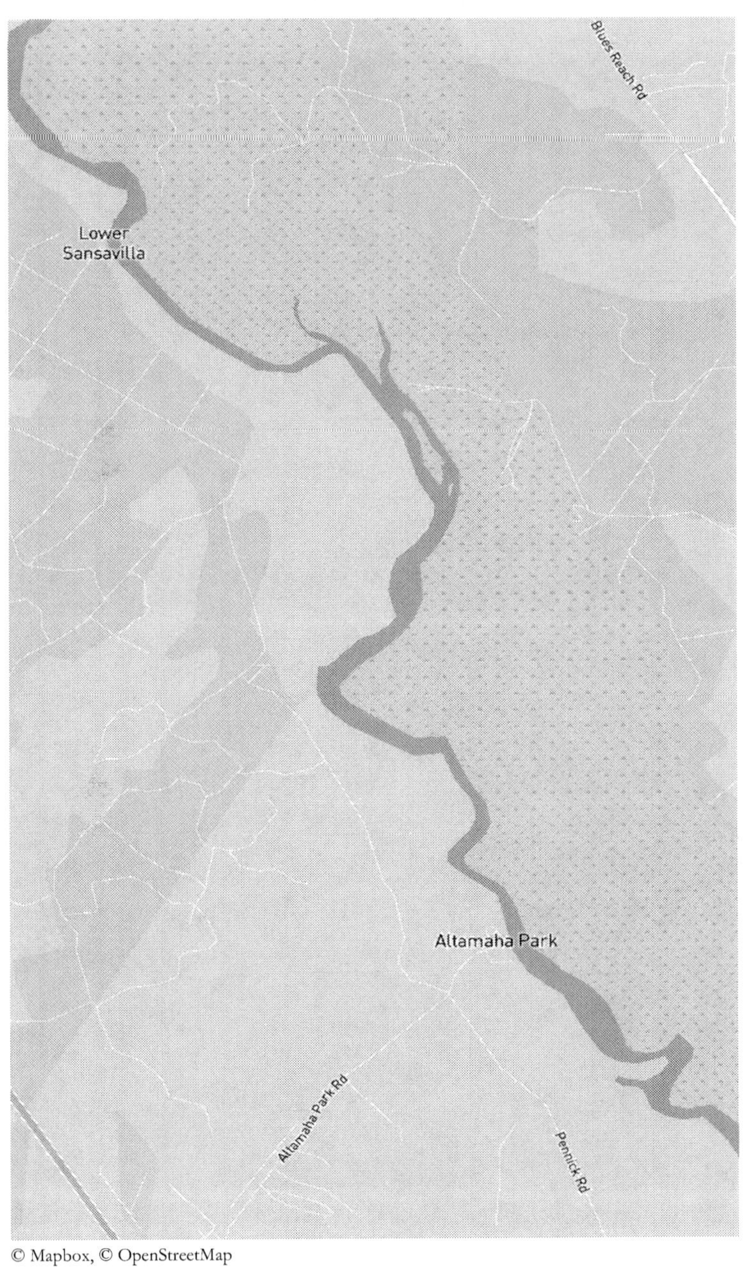
Blues Reach Rd
Lower
Sansavilla
Altamaha Park
Altamaha Park Rd
Pennick Rd

Day XXI

Gator Throwing

I caught an alligator with Tyler this morning! Today was the first time I was in a canoe with Tyler the whole trip. There would have been no other person I would have attempted to catch an alligator with. It had to have been a divine set up. Our canoe was in the lead. As soon as I saw it, I knew it was catchable; too small and its mom would have been around, too big, and it could have torn us to pieces.

When we paddled toward the right side of the river, it ran into a little flood-pond on the other side of the bank. We spotted him after almost giving up the search and devised a plan. Tyler was more confident than I was, but I told him if anyone was going to grab the head, it was going to be me. The last thing I wanted was to pry the gator's jaws off his hand. I would much rather my hand get hurt than his.

Before we made our move, the alligator sprinted for the river. A chase ensued. The gator hit our beached canoe which slowed him enough for Tyler to reach him before the gator made it to the water. Tyler grabbed his tail and flung him back on land, toward me. I closed the gap between the alligator and the river, stepped on his back, then put my hand around his neck. We had him!

He was impressively strong when he tried to wiggle free. I held on as tight as I could. He squeaked over and over. I told myself that he was too big for mom to still be around. Finally, he calmed down, but his mouth remained open waiting for a finger to slip between his jaws. By now the other four canoes had landed a little downriver from us. A few saw the series of events leading up to the capture. Others were oblivious to what was going on.

Tyler and I showed off our catch to the group. Everyone got a chance to hold him. Most took advantage of the opportunity to hold a wild alligator. Disposable waterproof cameras flashed scenes of life-jacketed boys nervously smiling as they gripped the midsection and tail. My left hand always held the neck. We observed the alligator had five toes on his front feet and four on the back. (I keep calling the alligator a "he," but I have no idea. We didn't check.) The rear feet had webbed toes. He wasn't slimy as some of the boys suspected. We released him, and he scurried into the water. All of us were in shock at what just happened. Never had I imagined we would be able to catch an alligator on the side of the Altamaha.

An hour later, we reached the Altamaha Fish Camp Landing. We emptied trash, filled jerry jugs, then explored. We walked through a nature trail on the north side. On the way, we saw huge palmettos a few feet off the trail. Some of the guys took pictures by them as a reference to show their size. Right after that, we heard rustling in the woods and saw an armadillo. Further down the trail we stopped to play around large cypress trees and found a wasp dragging a huge spider up a tree. It didn't mind us watching its struggle to get it up to where we suspected its nest was.

Back on the river, we felt the effects of the tide for the first time. It wasn't helping our speed and was continuously getting stronger in the other direction. We inched along in the hot sun searching for a campsite. The river widened, and no sandbars were found. The banks became higher, too high for us to lift all our gear to shore. The thick trees went straight to the bank's edge and seemed uninviting for camping. Seemingly miles of unbending river deteriorated our spirit. But we pushed onward. There weren't many complaints for us to stop because the boys had learned how to determine a good campsite. There were none!

Around 4:15 p.m., we saw a clear elevated area to the left and honed our canoes toward the spot. It took so long to reach. Stroke after stroke, the clear area didn't seem to be getting any closer. It felt like we were going absolutely nowhere. My strength was starting to fade, so I knew the boys were running low on muscle and motivation too. Shouting out encouragements and with thoughts of halting our paddling for the day, we kept our strokes consistent. Finally, we made it. Though it was tough I enjoyed the difficulty. It's good to be exhausted after a hard day's work, knowing you gave it your all.

We took one look at it and knew it would suffice for the night. We didn't want to get back on the river with no way of knowing where the next decent spot would show up on the horizon. There was a small cove that could protect our canoes, but it was big enough for only one canoe to unload at a time. The rain runoff had washed out a piece of the bank, making a path up to the level upper area. This route was the only way we could reach the top. Other people had camped here before. Large amounts of trash were scattered around. Broken chairs, small propane tanks, and even a bulky piece of carpet were strewn here. We cleared out the trash as best as we could and stomped down the weeds. A few of the guys helped me pull the carpet back so we could have enough room to set up our tents.

The *Hunger Games* is super addicting. I'll need to start reading after the boys go to bed so I can pay attention to what is going on in the group. This evening I was reading after supper while the boys were working on academics and fishing. For a majority of the time, I was unaware of much going on beside what was between the pages of my book. I finished First Samuel tonight in chief's tent after the boys went to bed. Chief Travis brought out some beef jerky he had gotten in a package at resupply. It was amazing! The best jerky I think I've ever had!

9:16 p.m.

Group Journal: Day 21

"Good Morning!" said Chief Mike. After he said that, everyone popped up and got ready for the day we had planned. We took down tents. We did an okay job at that. Then we ate and got on the river by nine. That was awesome. After about thirty minutes into it, we saw an alligator and we caught it. That was awesome. Then after that we had lunch at a fishing camp. After lunch the group walked around for a little while. We were walking around. We had seen us some armadillos in the woods. That was cool because that was the first time I seen one of those in the wild. Then after that we headed back out to find us a campsite. We were on the river for a long time before finding a campsite. When we got to our campsite, we unpacked and moved out quick. Then we had dinner and then went to pow-wow to end off our awesome day.

Oh. Some other things we had done was fishing. No one caught anything. We also saw some awesome trucks with nice lift kits. And about our campsite, it was very small but we managed with it. Well, that's about it for day twenty-one.

Logan

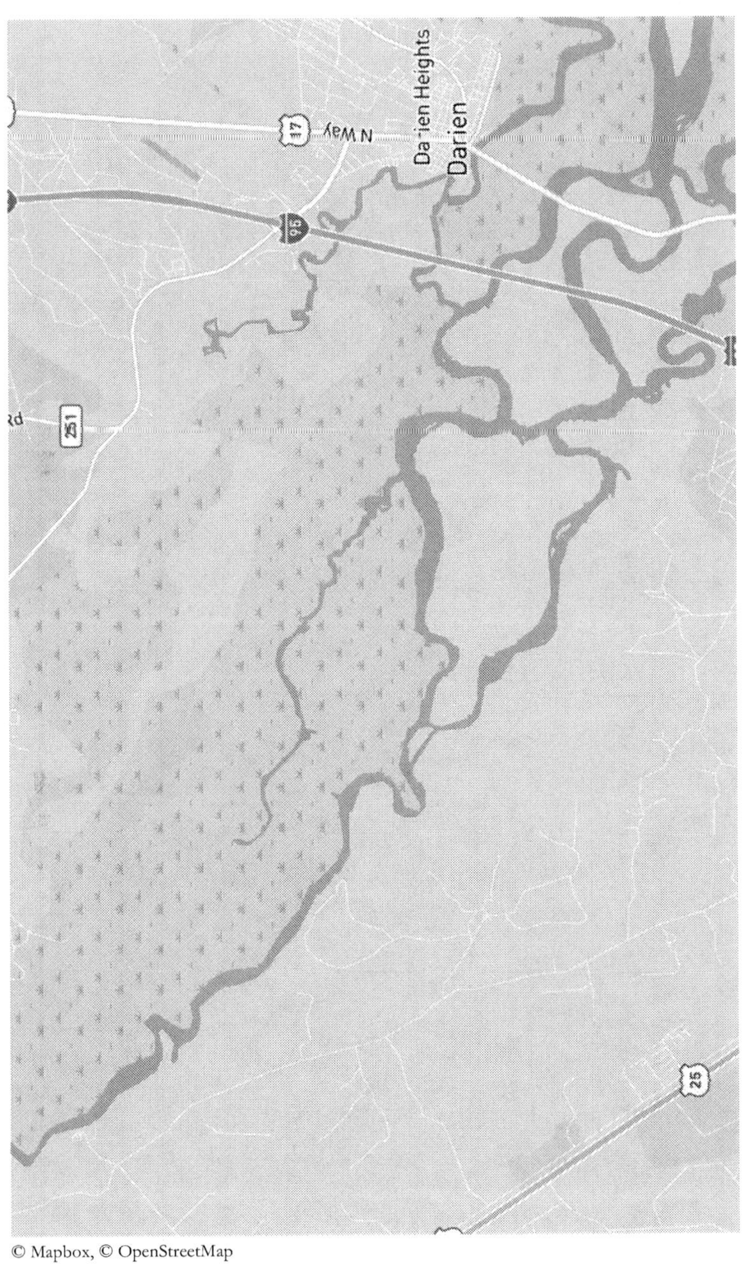

© Mapbox, © OpenStreetMap

Day XXII

Little Man

Last night, after I was in my sleeping bag and had just finished journaling, Zach started yelling, "Chief! Chief!" I got out of the tent to check on him and realized he was sleep talking. Since I was already out of the tent, I thought I might as well use the bathroom. About the time I turned around to go back into the tent, I felt an intense pain in my right foot. I shined my headlight down to see my foot engulfed in fire ants. I let out a few choice words and beat the ants off. I imagine I had between fifty and seventy-five ants on my foot. They were so strategic not to bite until all of them were ready to bite in unison.

The pain wouldn't go away and was too excruciating to sleep, so I read the *Hunger Games* for an hour or so until the pain died down. When we rolled the carpet up, we exposed a huge fire ant colony. Fortunately, no tents pitched over it. I told the story to the boys at breakfast; they all rolled around laughing.

What a day! We packed up and ate quickly so we could catch the tide on its way out. There's no way we wanted to start off today going against the tide. Getting on the river by 8:15 a.m. was our solution to use the tide to our advantage. It felt good and would give us time to explore downstream.

Yesterday we had gotten a tide chart at the Altamaha Fish Camp Landing. I'm glad we did. If we would have just tried to fight through it or try to get lucky with the tide, we would have been hurting by the end of the day. In addition to our sore muscles, we wouldn't have made many miles, and our morale would have plummeted.

Fifteen minutes on the river, the boys couldn't hold their secret anymore. I gave the signal, and all of the canoes circled Chief Travis's canoe. Once we closed in on a thoroughly confused Chief Travis, we sang happy birthday. Full of smiles, he thanked us, and we continued on our way. The river continued to widen. I looked at the map last night to see numerous channels and outlets. We needed to stay on the left to reach Darien. There were two bridges we passed today to help confirm our position. The first bridge was Interstate 95. The second was Highway 17. If we saw the town of Darien to our left, it would solidify we had canoed to the right spot.

In Darien we passed all sorts of shrimp boats. They were bigger than any boats we had seen on the river, and the biggest some of the boys had ever seen. I was in the front canoe taking time to look at the different vessels but also trying to keep a decent pace. Every so often, I looked behind and noticed the group getting farther and farther apart. Chad and I stopped on the left side of the river and watched a bird with a colorful head fishing for minnows within ten feet of the bow of the canoe. Chief Mike and Jaylen's canoe seemed to stop. Chad and I watched the bird attempt to get his lunch for fifteen minutes, and they hadn't gotten any closer. Jaylen started waving frantically. I couldn't hear him, but we turned the rest of the fleet around to meet him.

Once we reached Jaylen's canoe, we saw a man standing on the boat above him. Jaylen had asked the man if we could take a look at his boat. The boys' faces all lit up when he revealed the news. The gentleman told us we could tie our canoes to a boat farther down, climb aboard, and make our way to the dock. We ventured our way over and hopped from boat to boat until we reached the dock. We then walked over to the man's boat but had to jump a rundown boat before setting our feet on his vessel. We quickly went around and introduced ourselves. We found out the gentleman's name was Greg Boone. We were on the Little Man, named for his son.

Greg was a thin man in his late forties or early fifties who wore a white collared shirt. We still had our lifejackets on because we didn't anticipate staying long. Mr. Boone asked questions about who we were and what we were doing canoeing down the river. We told him a little about camp and our adventures so far. He seemed genuinely interested. The conversation turned to his boat, and he started telling us how the shrimp boat works and giving us information about the area. Ironically he is allergic to shrimp. Greg even has to wear gloves while handling them. He told us about jelly balls. They're orange-pink balls that are the size of a softball. They feel like hard jellyfish. They're used by food companies as filler food to absorb and mimic the flavor.

We ended up staying for three hours talking about the shrimping business, his family life, and whatever else we could think of to ask. He was so open with everything. His father started the family business sixty years ago. After explaining almost everything on the vessel, he treated us to vanilla ice cream. It was the first thing cold that has touched my lips in three weeks. It was euphoric! We ate it out of little plastic cups and savored every bite. This all came to be because Jaylen was bold enough to ask Mr. Boone if we could see his boat.

Mr. Boone got off the boat with us, and we made a quick stop back by our canoes to get our Nalgenes and lunch.

Since we stayed later than expected, we decided to eat lunch in Darien. We walked with Mr. Boone, and he showed us where they ice and box the shrimp. He offered to give us ice for our water bottles. It doesn't get much better than an iced drink on a hot day. I've missed the luxury of having a drink that's cooler than the temperature outside. Before saying goodbye Mr. Boone pointed us in the direction of the town's welcome center. It turned out to be the Chamber of Commerce which was equal in usefulness.

I called Fort King George while the rest went to an art museum located in an old prison. I ran the mile to the fort so I could talk with the park manager face-to-face. I always feel like I'm more likely to get help if I'm there in person. Mr. Steven Smith, the park manager, let us stay inside the fort for free. He even drove me back to the Chamber of Commerce so I could meet back up with the group.

I then walked to the museum and was surprised by how interesting it was. It was all local/historical art which helped paint a more vivid picture of the area. I'm happy we're getting a good feel for the culture around the river. The boys have seen good southern hospitality throughout the trip. We've learned about rafting and shrimping, and now we're learning about Darien's history before the Civil War. At 4:15 p.m., a few minutes after I arrived, the lady behind the desk kindly asked us to leave and closed up fifteen minutes late. We thanked her for showing us around. Hopefully, we can go back tomorrow.

While making our way back to the dock and to our canoes, Mr. Boone stopped us and gave us three loaves of bread and ten pounds of chicken. Fresh meat! The freezer where he got the chicken was located in a small white shed close to his shop. In the shed, there were pictures of his family and a small table with chairs surrounding it. On the left side after coming in there were several caviar tins. I had no idea caviar was sturgeon eggs and could fetch so much money per ounce. Mr. Boone told us of all the regulations for caviar and said it wasn't a big business. We were profoundly thankful for the chicken. Chief Travis got ice cream and grilled chicken for his birthday!

We made our way to Fort King George, which wasn't far. On the way, we saw four dolphins in the distance. When we reached the fort, we unpacked our gear and put it in the grass as close to the dock as possible without it being in anyone's way. At Fort King George, we cooked the chicken in a pre-civil war style oven inside the fort. It tasted phenomenal. Potted meat and beef jerky cannot compare to the luxurious chicken. We haven't gotten to check out much of the fort yet. It is by far the most mosquito-infested campsite we have had. I heard it will get worse as we reach the islands. Mr. Boone was surprised when we told him we didn't bring along special candles that ward away the pests.

Half an hour after the boys went down, Will thought he heard chains and the clanging around of a ghost in the old fort and hollered for a chief. I stuck half my body out of the tent and reassured him that nothing was going to bother him. Within the thirty seconds, it took me to talk with Will, a swarm of mosquitoes latched onto me and poured into the tent. I spent the next several minutes swatting, and by the time all the mosquitoes perished, my hands were covered in blood.

11:02 p.m.

Group Journal: Day 22

Today was a good day. We woke up and got in a good gather up and got ready to take down tents. After that, we got ready by loading canoes and eating breakfast. We wanted to be on the river early so that we could beat the tide. This morning we got on the river by 8:15am. After ten minutes passed by, we sang happy birthday to Chief Travis aka Chief Deazle. Today I want to, well not just me, the group wants to make it a special day for him. So we paddled real hard to get to Darien. When we got there, we saw a lot of very big boats. They had cool names like Gravedigger, Cat'sass, and Little Man. That was the first time I ever seen a big boat like that even though it was a shrimp boat. We met a man named Mr. Boone. He is a really nice man. He showed us around on his boat.

I thought it was cool that he would show strangers around on his boat. His boat was the Little Man. He has a family-owned shrimp place. He showed us things about his boat and gave us ice cream. I had a big smile on my face because I've never been on a big boat, and I saw things I probably would have never seen before. After that, he took us on a little tour on the docks and showed us what he does and told us more about his life and his family and how things work. Mr. Boone gave the group some ice for our water bottles and told us more about the river. He gave us some very good chicken and I thought that was cool because Chief Travis got ice cream and chicken for his birthday.

Later, after a fun lunch, we went back to our canoes and went up river. We found out that we are staying at Fort King George. On the way, we saw four dolphins swimming next to our canoes. Ten minutes later we arrived at our campsite. It was the best. We walked around and had a good dinner and got ready for bed. I think this is a lifetime trip and that Chief Travis had a good birthday, and then we went to bed. The end.

Robert

Boonedocks

The tide was high early in the morning and flowing down stream with us. It wasn't going to be with us all morning, so we rushed to get on the Altamaha River. 8:00am was the time we got off from shore, which was about an hour earlier than we have been setting off during this trip. This particular morning, we only had ten miles to go to reach Darien, Geogria. Darien was our pick up point, but today was not our day to be picked up. We were three or four days ahead of schedule, which left us plenty of time for the events of the rest of the day.

We reached Darien around 10:00am and were admiring all the different shrimp boats. The last boats in the docks had a few guys on them and we waved. We turned around and went by again and Jaylen yelled out to one of the men, "Can we get a tour of your boat?" The man we got to know well as Greg Boone replied from his Boonedocks, "Yeah! I think I got some ice cream for you all also."

We tied up on one of his boats and hopped over to the "Little Man" which was actually one of the bigger shrimp boats in Darien. This boat was named after Greg's son's nickname. From the deck of the boat, Greg opened the hatch to show us the iced storage spaces below where they keep all the shrimp fresh while they are out for days dragging their nets. From there, he took us into the cabin of the boat, turned on the radar and GPS and showed us all his markings from the waters. He had good spots marked, bad spots, and hangs where he found wreckage and tore his nets.

After showing us around, Greg Boone got out the ice cream that was donated by some churches to the fishermen. We hadn't tasted anything so cold in weeks; weeks of upper-ninety degree weather. While cooling off to the ice cream, Greg talked with us for three hours telling us everything from him growing up eleven years old on the shrimp boats to the Discovery Channel making a show on his sixty year family shrimping business. The show will be called Muddy Water with one of the boonedock songs as the theme song.

Greg talked to the group of twelve of us on his shrimp boat about the history of the Altamaha River and shrimping business that his grandpa started. He told us about costs of everything on the boat and different prices he can get for shrimp explaining why it is not profitable for him to be out fishing right now with small numbers of shrimp within range. He talked to us about government issues, family issues, and safety issues all dealing with shrimping.

From the deck of the boat, he took us to the warehouse inland where they package the shrimp and gave us ice for our water that had become scalding hot. We left our canoes tied up to his boats and went walking through town. Darien is a town of great history and many other people that want to help.

When we got back to the Boonedocks, Greg was there and gave us ten pounds of frozen chicken and three loaves of bread, while he showed us more pictures and told us more stories for another half hour.

Greg is one of the many amazing people we met on the river. He is a man that taught us so much that inspired and entertained all of us. One thing that Greg and many others taught us is that we shouldn't hesitate to ask from people on the river because they are happy to give.

Chief Mike

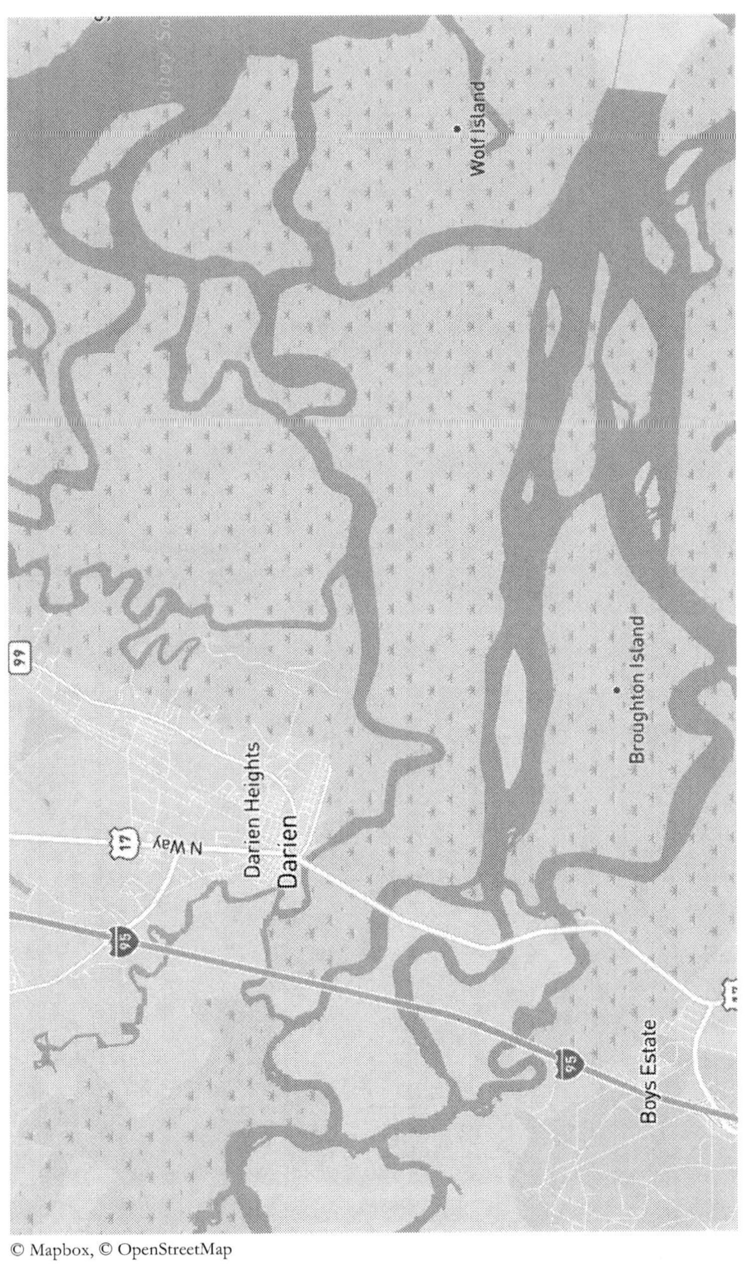

Wolf Island
Broughton Island
Darien Heights
Darien
N Way
17
99
95
Boys Estate

Day XXIII

Darien

Today was a layover day. Before we went anywhere, we packed up our tents quickly and moved our gear close to the dock. Visitors would be coming to the fort, and we did not want any of our things in the way. When we finished, we could barely make out the four squares of flattened grass where our tents were. The boys were able to take showers this morning too. I took mine last night. It was a good opportunity to relax, shave, and decompress a little. Logan and I had virtually the same clothes on. We both had similar khaki shorts and lime green shirts on. We looked like brothers and took a picture together to commemorate our wardrobe selection.

We went to the front desk and asked if there was anything we could do to help. Mr. Smith had prepared a few things for us to do. One project was to do a task we do all the time at camp—clean up a woodpile. We've gotten lucky to receive such compatible projects to compensate staying at places along the river. They've been similar to what we do at camp.

First, we had to pick up pinecones and now stack wood. We stacked all the fallen wood and consolidated the little piles into a straight line about four feet high. We also cleaned the bathrooms and restocked them with paper towels and toilet paper.

Finished with our work, we checked out the museum attached to the welcome center. We saw what uniforms looked like during the time period the fort was functioning. The boys read about medical practices and fatalities. We walked outside and went into the fort. There we imagined we were at war, firing the cannons and preparing for battle.

Following our tour of the museum and grounds, we walked to the art museum we were at yesterday by a more scenic route. Before we got to the renovated prison, we ate lunch at the tiny town square, which the boys thought was a weird name for the location. The square was circular. For lunch, we had individual cans of tuna. Only a few people brought plier tools with can openers so several had to wait until we passed them around. We all waited until the last can was open before we ate.

The art at Old Jail Art Center & Museum was amazing. I was disappointed I wasn't able to spend much time there yesterday. Photographic art took up all the space on the staircase and was my favorite. I've always admired the skill of taking breathtaking landscapes and inspirational natural scenes. The amount of detail on the cloth napkin and the apples on one of the paintings was incredible. Since most of the art was from local artists, the boys were able to get a unique taste of southern culture through means we don't normally explore.

The gallery was run solely by volunteers. One volunteer was able to give us a little history about the displays. On the wall, I admired *The Old Soup Pot.* This artist was a genius with colored pencils. On a wooden table a colorful dish towel was underneath a few apples, and a pot turned on its side. The detail on the towel was both simple and majestic; the blue and red and yellow stripes on the white cloth bent with the folds and faded in the unlit portions of the drawing. Upstairs the jail cells were kept intact but were filled with displays of the town's history.

When we saw all we could see, we retraced our steps back to the park to meet Carlton Morrison, the author of *Running the River*[7], a historical guide book we purchased at the Towns Bluff Landing. I got his number from Ms. Anna and called to see if he'd be willing to meet with us. He shared stories about rafting and pole-boating on the river. His explanation painted a more vivid picture for the boys. I couldn't imagine going upstream hundreds of miles using a crew of ten men equipped only with poles. In those days, they would form a line of five on each side of the boat then reach their pole to the bottom and walk forward while the frontman went to the back of the vessel. While Mr. Morrison talked with us, a lady sat to the side taking notes. She heard about us and wanted to write an article for the local paper. Some of the boys were quoted, and we all posed for a picture.

After Mr. Morrison and the lady from the newspaper left, we walked around Darien again. Chiefs scoped out a good spot to be picked up from our journey. We wanted the supervisor picking us up to have no trouble finding us. Along the way, we came across some tabby buildings. Tabby is a type of cement of equal parts of water, lime, sand, and seashells. The "ruins" were from the 1820s.

Right now, I'm in the barracks fanning mosquitoes away from my face and arms. We abandoned our tents to sleep here just to say we slept in barracks that people slept in before the Revolutionary War. I'm sad to say I was the biggest proponent on creating the excitement of staying in the barracks. The mosquitoes are terribly annoying, but I think it will be worth it to say that we slept here. I mean, who can say they slept in a pre-Revolutionary War fort?

A storm seems to be rolling in. We can see the lightning flash every few minutes. Chief Travis and I pulled all the canoes out of the water and turned them over after pow-wow to prevent the storm from capsizing or filling them with water. The tide also posed a problem. When my group was on the Suwannee River on the gulf side of Florida, we made the mistake of tying our canoes to the dock when we were at the mouth of the river. The next morning, when we went to get the canoes, they had floated under the dock, and the tide trapped them. It was time-consuming getting them unstuck.

Hopefully, we can spend the night on an island tomorrow.

Group Journal: Day 23

Today the Rangers were exploring the things in the town of Darien. While we were in Darien, we took showers so that we could smell really good. We got to go back to the old jail art museum. We also got to see Mr. Carlton Morrison. Before we saw Mr. Carlton, we got to see some plums growing on a tree and we got to see crabapples growing on a tree. Another amazing thing that happened today is that we solved a problem.

When we woke up this morning we took showers and we also did our service project. Our service project was like the normal thing that we do at camp, and it was stacking wood in a neat pile. Another thing that we learned was that Fort King George was burned and rebuilt. We also got to learn that Carlton Morrison's father was on a raft. When Carlton Morrison was talking to us, there was a lady who was writing things down about what she heard.

Yesterday we also walked around Darien. When we were walking we went to go look at the signs that were in Darien.

This morning we had packed up our tents because people were coming to see the fort. When we were looking at the fort, we saw some things that we never seen before. We got to see where they stored their ammo and their gun powder. We also learned that the six-pound cannon balls went a mile when they were shot out of the cannon. We also learned that the Indians lived on the fort when it was there.

Jaylen

Darien

Darien is a popular fishing place on the east coast. This year there is not a lot of fish or shrimp. In Darien at a small boat dock, there is a man named Greg Boone. He let me and my group, the Rangers, come aboard his ship. While we were aboard the ship, Mr. Greg showed us every part of the ship and told us what it was. After he showed us the ship, we sat on his top deck and talked about old stories.

Another reason why Darien is popular is because of their wood. People built rafts and put them in the river. They floated from Macon all the way to Darien where they took the rafts apart and loaded them in ships. The ships took them all round the world to different countries. It started in 1888 and ended in the early 1900s.

In Darien there is a fort. The name of the fort is Fort King George. My group got to stay and camp out in the fort. It was a cool experience. Near the fort, there used to be an Indian tribe, the Guale, that moved and never returned. The fort kept all the pottery and used it in everyday life. There was a man named Carlton Morrison who came. He's the one who told me about the rafts. Darien was awesome and I cannot wait for the next place to learn some more.

Will

Day XXIV

Voyage to Sapelo

Throughout last night, Caleb was constantly by my side, saying he couldn't handle the mosquitoes. I kept spraying him with bug spray in vain. I told him to try to get some sleep despite the buzzing, biting, and the sound of others swatting. It sounded like the group was practicing a drum line routine. Though it was unbearably hot, everyone got in their sleeping bags to avoid the swarm. Inside my sleeping bag, I felt as if I would shrivel up like a raisin due to so much water loss. I don't know what was worse: the heat or the mosquitoes. I couldn't wait for sunrise.

Everyone related to the retelling of my miserable night last night. Chief Travis and Logan were the only ones who weren't bothered in the barracks. They were on the top bunk and had pushed open the wooden windows. This kept a steady breeze flowing over them and kept the nuisance mosquitoes away. No one else was as fortunate to be by an open window facing the ocean.

We left Fort King George this morning after cleaning a little more around the place. We emptied all the trash cans around the property. We mopped the bathroom floors and vacuumed the museum and theatre. Outside, a closet with all sorts of cleaning supplies and miscellaneous items needed organized. It was great for the boys to serve. No one complained. The boys with me took everything off the shelves and threw away empty containers. We consolidated trash bags and rubber gloves into a few manageable boxes. Then we wiped everything clean. We finished the job by categorizing the items so they'd be easy to find.

We were advised by the park manager to go south of Sapelo Island but not to go to the reserve island. Permission to camp on the barrier island is required. The island can only be accessed by boat or plane. A daily ferry runs residents to the mainland. Permission is obtained by knowing a resident of the island or going with an organized tour. From Fort King George, we headed toward the coast.

Originally the tide wasn't too bad, but near the end, the current turned, and paddling grew tiresome. The turning tide lost our attention for a moment when we saw the sky grow eerily grey and felt the wind pick up. The chiefs had a direction in mind; we wanted to find a few specific islands we intended to stay the night at. We turned the corner and saw the islands that were camp-able without having a permit. There were virtually no trees. No trees meant no deadwood for starting cooking fires and also meant no palce to hang tarps. There was hardly any vegetation at all, just razor-sharp rock beaches with grass poking up near the middle of the island. Sapelo was within viewing distance with its orange and white striped lighthouse. Quickly weighing our options, I pointed the nose of the canoe toward the forbidden island.

By then, the tide was in full force going inland, and the storm was approaching from the southeast. Impending storms never bothered us as much as this one did today. The wind blew swiftly, doubling the effort needed to get to shore. The extra-large canoe was taking on water regularly with the big waves flowing over the gunwales. I prayed that Mitchell and I didn't tump. Though we were millimeters from dipping the gunwales into the ocean, we never capsized. Both of us had to paddle fiercely on our left to reach our destination. If we switched sides, the momentum from our paddle strokes would have tipped the canoe and sent us into the ocean. Lightning flickered behind us.

Mitchell kept yelling back to me that his arm was cramping and that he was too exhausted to go on. I yelled encouragements over the wind and waves and silently prayed that we would make it to land without disaster. "This is where we become strong, Mitchell," "I believe in you," We're almost there." Some of the group saw a blacktip shark investigating the five slender canoes from twenty yards away. Mitchell either didn't see it or was too scared to acknowledge it.

Our focal point on Sapelo was the edge of the island facing the ocean. It was the closest part of the island to us, where the sandy beach was located. Unfortunately, this was also the hardest point to reach with the wind and the tide.

Instead of keeping the course for the island's edge, Mitchell and I turned left toward to the lighthouse to see if we could shore our canoes there until the wind died down and the tide withdrew to the ocean. The lighthouse was further west on the island. While the waves would still be a hindrance, we'd have a little help from the tide. We reached the shore, but found only a rocky marsh unsuitable for landing. We would've had to carry all our supplies and canoes several hundred yards across treacherous rocks. Mitchell and I shoved back into the water, waving the others off our course. Now we had a lot of ground to make up, and we had to go straight against the tide rather than having the tide push the side of the canoe.

We crept along at a snail's pace, the wind blasting warm air in our faces. Thankfully, Mitchell and I were able to paddle on the other side of our canoe, but our jobs were no easier than before. We were fighting the tide head-on. Several of the boys had their heads down, focusing on every stroke. I was worried about Chief Mike's canoe. It was taking on a lot of water. I'm not sure if it was the one that started leaking when Logan and Jaylen got stuck on a log in the middle of the river on day sixteen. Even if it wasn't the same canoe, the waves and weight in the canoe were more than enough to cause problems. Zach was designated to scoop the water out because he was in cargo. He used a plastic cup he found earlier in the day. We saw the two paddles furiously going into the water, but they did not seem to be getting any closer to shore. If anyone tumped they would be carried away by the tide and investigated by the blacktips.

Tyler and Will made it before Mitchell and I finally hit the sandy shore. They were out of their canoe, waving us on, watching all the drama unfold on the water. Everyone who landed shouted support for those still working against the wind and waves. Slowly but surely, the bows of the canoes ran onto the shoreline. While I saw several exhausted faces, I couldn't find a frown among the group. We successfully completed a task I'm sure none of them thought we could accomplish without incurring some sort of disaster.

As soon as everyone came to shore, we unloaded canoes and set up tents. It was close to 2:00 p.m., and we had not eaten lunch. We put the canoes in between tents and ran ropes across the canoes and tents to brace for what we thought would be a significant storm. After that, we changed into swimsuits to avoid getting our clothes wet. We ate our meal in anticipation of the rain. Above both sides of our campsite, telltale streaks in the sky signified rain.

It never came. We were dry. God helped us out again. Following the meal, we rambled in search of shells and other beach artifacts. Logan found a live horseshoe crab. A few of the others caught hermit crabs. While cooks prepared the meal, the rest fished and worked on academics. I finished the first *Hunger Games* book.

We heard from Greg Boone and Mr. Smith that the mosquitoes were worse on the islands. I was prepared to get in the tent quickly and not get out unless I absolutely had to. Surprisingly it was a stark difference from the night before. I barely got any sleep last night. The mosquitoes in the barracks were terrible. I tried to keep myself in my sleeping bag, but I roasted. Now I am slightly chilled and haven't encountered a single mosquito.

Hard circumstances reveal character. We talked about the changing character in ourselves and in our group throughout the trip and especially today. During our trials this afternoon we all did our part from Zach scooping water out, to the paddlers refusing to crumble under pressure, to those who made it to shore giving encouragements over the wind rather than laughing at others' struggles.

8:39 p.m.

I can hear the thunder of another approaching storm.

Group Journal: Day 24

Today was exciting because last night we got to sleep in a fort called Fort King George which was sweet. The only problem with that was the mosquitoes in the fort's bunkers were even worse than outside, and that is bad. So in the morning everyone had mosquito bites all over them which was funny to me because everyone had them all over their bodies. Ha ha. Anyway, we packed our sleeping bags and took our breaks, and the manager had asked us if we could help him out with a job or two, and so we said yes since he let us stay completely free of charge.

The first job was to clean the bathrooms, which there were three but he said just to clean two out of the three, and the second job was to clean out and put back the stuff that was in a closet. So the first job: the bathrooms. The first bathroom it was Chief Travis, Caleb, Robert, and I double tag-teamed it. It was me on the sinks and mirrors, Robert had the toilets, and Chief Travis and Caleb sweeped. Then we vacuumed the fort's museum and the theaters and mopped the floor. The same was in the women's bathroom, but it was easier to clean than the men's. I really loved helping. So then we got in the canoes and headed to the coast. The waves were so sweet man. I loved it.

Zach

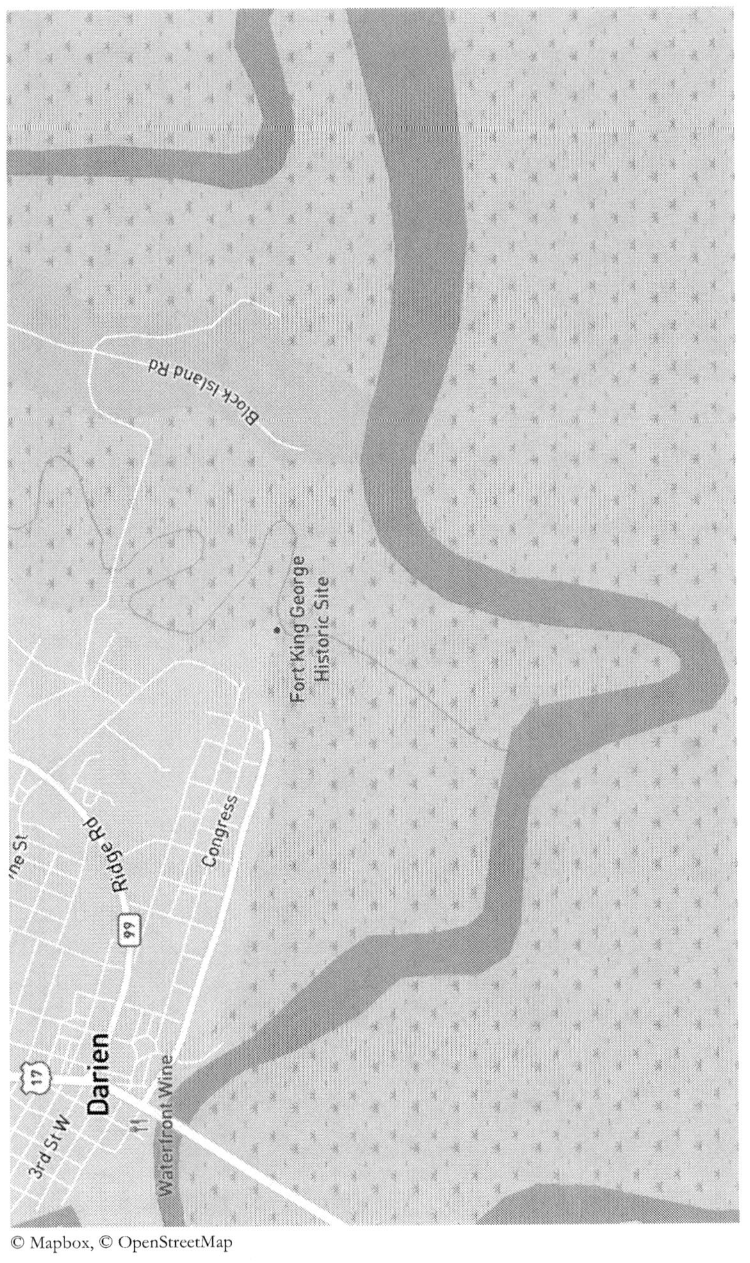

© Mapbox, © OpenStreetMap

Day XXV

Sand Dollars & Jelly Balls

This morning we packed up our tents and loaded the canoes before eating our cold breakfast. While folding our tents, a few of us caught glimpses of ghost crabs hiding underneath the ground tarps that lay between the sand and our tents. Today, even though we were packed and ready we didn't get in the canoes until after lunch. The tide changed around that time, and we used it to our advantage. I am thankful we picked up a tide chart at the Altamaha Fish Camp Landing. It would have been miserable to go against it again.

Rambling around the beach seemed like the best option to occupy our time before the tide changed. Before walking the beach, we packed up everything we had so we could leave quickly when it was time to go. I'd rather work first and play later, although loading canoes doesn't seem like work to me anymore. I don't think it does to the boys either.

The ramble was well worth it. Almost immediately, we began finding treasures. Boys pulled hermit crabs from the water. A few horseshoe crabs were captured by flipping them over or picking up their tail. One of the boys found a string of tiny shells. I have no idea what it was, but it looked beautiful, like a mermaid's lost necklace.

I stepped on a stingray within thirty feet of our campsite. It felt like a slimy tire. Luckily, it didn't send its barb through my heel. Even though we already discussed shuffling our feet, the incident reemphasized the importance without a word. Stepping on one scared me enough to walk on the sand for a while. Some of the boys followed me out of the water.

Tyler jumped into the water after a blacktip shark. He said he touched its tail, but I have a hard time believing him. After turning the corner to the East toward the open ocean, several of the boys found unbroken sand dollars. Once the boys got an eye for finding them, they ran all trying to be the first to spot one. We also found the jelly balls Mr. Boone talked about. They were bigger than baseballs. A few of the boys amused themselves by seeing how far they could throw them into the ocean.

Mitchell was one of the last ones to find a pristine sand dollar. While Mitchell ran to show the group his find, he fell, breaking his perfect sand dollar. The other boys attempted to give him one of theirs. He wouldn't accept. He wanted to find one himself. I kept my eye out for another one. When I did, I secretly made sure Mitchell found it.

By the time we returned to our campsite, most of the boys' sand dollars had cracked. A few clutched their finds too hard. Others seemed not to care and took no precaution to protect the fragile object. Hopefully, no more of them break. My two are rolled up with a few of my clothes.

It's Sunday today, so I asked the boys to sit with me. We sat with the sun and wind in our faces. I told them the story of the boy and the old man who went walking along the beach filled with beached starfish. It was a story I was told by a French youth in New Orleans in a Hurricane Katrina relief workers' camp. It made an impact on my life, and what a perfect setting to set the stage for the story this morning. I told the guys that our actions, like the boy's actions in the story, make a significant impact. Starfish can represent right actions in a world of poor decisions. Pursuing what is right even when it's unpopular or feels overwhelming is something we ought to do.

> One day a man was walking along the beach when he noticed a boy hurriedly picking up and gently throwing things into the ocean.
>
> Approaching the boy, he asked, "Young man, what are you doing?"
>
> The boy replied, "Throwing starfish back into the ocean. The surf is up and the tide is going out. If I don't throw them back, they'll die."
>
> The man chuckled and said, "Don't you realize there are miles and miles of beach and countless starfish? You can't make any difference!"
>
> After listening politely, the boy bend down, picked up another starfish, and threw it into the surf. Then, smiling at the man, he said,
>
> "I made a difference to that one."[8]

When we started making our way back from our ramble and impromptu chapel service, we noticed several boaters had come to our campsite's section of the beach. We made an effort to stay out of their way and divert our eyes from bikinis. After getting back to our gear, we checked everything and pushed the canoes into the ocean. We hit the tide just right and rode it back to Fort King George where we set up campsite for the night. On the way back we saw a few streaks of lightning. We were already going at a good pace, and there was no land to pull off at. There was nothing we could do but continue and hope the distant clouds did not come overhead. It sure looked like rain again, but God blessed us once more.

9:27 p.m.

It doesn't even need to be said that we did <u>not</u> spend tonight in the barracks.

Group Journal: Day 25

Good job guys! Keep it up! Last night was one of the best nights in a long time. There were no mosquitoes anywhere. The only thing we had to watch out for was any ghost crabs. When we got out and our tents were packed, the whole group started packing up the canoes. We got done in under twenty, maybe fifteen minutes. Then the cooks told us breakfast was ready. We had a wonderful meal of honey roasted peanuts and granola bars. Tyler was the first to drop out if there was not enough for a second helping.

Since we had a whole lot of energy, we decided to walk the beach. We found a whole lot of sand dollars and jelly balls. Tyler almost caught a shark, but the shark took off. When we headed back there was a group of people on the beach. Me and Logan went and checked on our crab cage to see if we caught anything. There was nothing in the cage, but we did get a bite. It took us the whole morning to walk the beach, so we decided to eat lunch. The lunch was about the same as the breakfast.

After lunch we scanned the ground and picked up anything that was on the ground, then got in a gather-up and chiefs told us who our canoe partners will be. My canoe partner was Robert. I was the bow, and Robert was my stern. When we got in the water it was calm, the tide was not going against us.

Me and Robert were the first to see Fort King George. As soon as we hit the docks, everyone started untying the canoes. After everything was unpacked, we ate dinner, then went to pow-wow. I like today because we got to explore and have fun.

Will

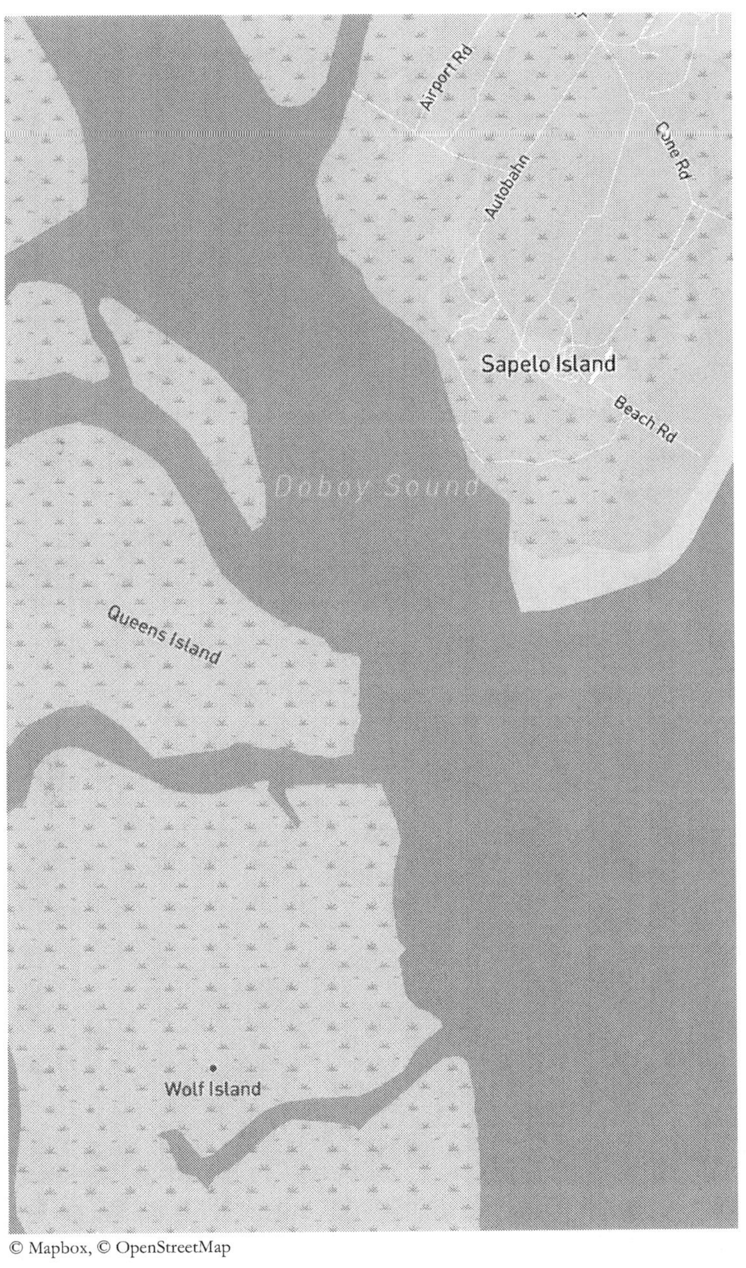
Airport Rd
Cane Rd
Autobahn
Sapelo Island
Beach Rd
Doboy Sound
Queens Island
Wolf Island

Day XXVI

Old Georgia

We planned to canoe upstream to the landing near the shrimp boats early this morning after we helped clean the fort for our final service project. We checked the grounds for trash and made sure the bathrooms were still in good condition. A few of us took trash to the dumpster. On the way, we saw our bus and trailer. I went to investigate and found our other supervisor, Chief Adam. He drove in last night, too late to come to our pitched tents inside the fort's walls. Chief Adam slept in the bus with his dog, Rosco. Since he was already at the fort, we decided to carry our canoes to the bus rather than canoe upriver and then load everything onto the bus from the landing.

Initially, I thought carrying everything to the bus would take longer, but it didn't take as long as I thought. We unloaded everything that was already packed in the canoes and hauled it two-hundred yards to the bus. Some of the boys thought they could carry a loaded canoe the entire way to the bus, but it proved too exhausting to continue. The boys were excited for our celebration. I'm sure that helped make the physically taxing effort easier. When everything was at the bus, we strategically loaded everything into the trailer with the big blue tarp underneath. The heavy items were placed in the middle, over the wheels, to balance the trailer. When everything was packed tightly, we folded the outside corners of the tarp inward to keep any rain out we may encounter then secured it with a few ropes. Then we got on Interstate 95 toward South Carolina. Before we crossed the border we sang *Old Georgia*, our rendition of *Old Texas*, for Chief Adam.

Old Georgia

I'm going to leave Old Georgia now
Ain't got no use for my canoe bow
We've paddled and steered the Altamaha
And the people there were all so kind
I'll take my rope, I'll take my painter
And leave them be, upon a tree
The soft, soft sand will be my bed
And my old roll-up will hold my head
I'll say "Bye ya'll" to the southerners
And turn the van 'tward Rangerland

Old Texas

I'm going to leave Old Texas Now
Ain't got no use for the long horned cow
They've plowed and fenced my cattle range
And the people there are all so strange
I'll take my horse, I'll take my rope
And hit the trail upon a lope
The hard, hard ground will be my bed
And the saddle seat will hold my head
I'll bid, "Adios" to the Alamo
And turn my head 'tward Mexico

Some of the boys complained of motion sickness after getting on the highway. It has been nearly a month since we've been in anything that goes over five miles per hour. Mail from camp was with Chief Adam, and he distributed it in the van. The boys were immersed in the letters from their parents. I set my two pristine sand dollars out to dry while Chief Adam drove. During the ride, both vibrated off the dash and chipped. I don't think anyone has a whole one anymore.

On big trips, we have the opportunity to celebrate after the journey. This usually includes traveling to a different location and celebrating our success with a fun activity. Celebrations should be on the way back to camp; it's hard to justify the cost of traveling father away from camp than the original trip. We also allot one meal to eat at the restaurant of our choice. This time we will head toward Huntington Beach State Park in South Carolina. We heard the white beaches are pristine. We prefer the most secluded campsites; the fewer distractions, the better.

About ten minutes from Huntington Beach State Park, another car got Chief Adam's attention and pointed to our trailer. The trailer had a flat tire. Thankfully, we didn't lose the trailer. Chief Mike noticed the leaf spring was broken. Somehow we were able to limp along slowly to the beach. Chief Adam called camp to fill Chief Jeremy, our maintenance man, in on the situation. He will have to come switch the trailers out.

I checked into the park and got our camping location. We found the tent camping sites and unloaded our gear. It was tight-fitting four tents in our space, but we had twenty-five days of practice. The group didn't think twice about the difficulty and made it work. This is Memorial Day Weekend. I would have assumed there would be a lot of music playing this evening, but it was peaceful when the sun sank below the trees. Thankfully, this place doesn't have many mosquitoes.

10:43 p.m.

Everyone is anticipating our glorious meal tomorrow. We get to eat at a buffet. I ate two helpings tonight to help stretch my stomach. I spent a fair amount of time reading on the four and a half-hour bus ride. I am in First Kings now, reading about Solomon.

Group Journal: Day 26

Today we woke up at Fort King George. It is our last day and a lot of people are sad to leave the river, but we all are excited to go to the beach. I am ready to go swimming. Chief Adam is going to pick us up at the fort. We had to carry our canoes and everything up to the bus. We did that very well. While we were riding to the campground our trailer spring broke and flattened our tire, so we had to replace it.

Our lunch was very, very good. We had Mountain Dew and cold cut sandwiches. What made them so good was that we have not had fresh food in a while, and it was good. After we had lunch and got the tire fixed, we was on our way to our campsite. After campsite was set-up. Cooks split off and we cooked jambalaya and dirt cake. It was a lot of food so we all got filled up on it.

Then we went to showers and got a whole new roll-up and we smelled a whole lot better than before. We went off to pow-wow and sang and had fun just talking about all of the fun that we have had on the trip and how proud we were of each other.

Tyler

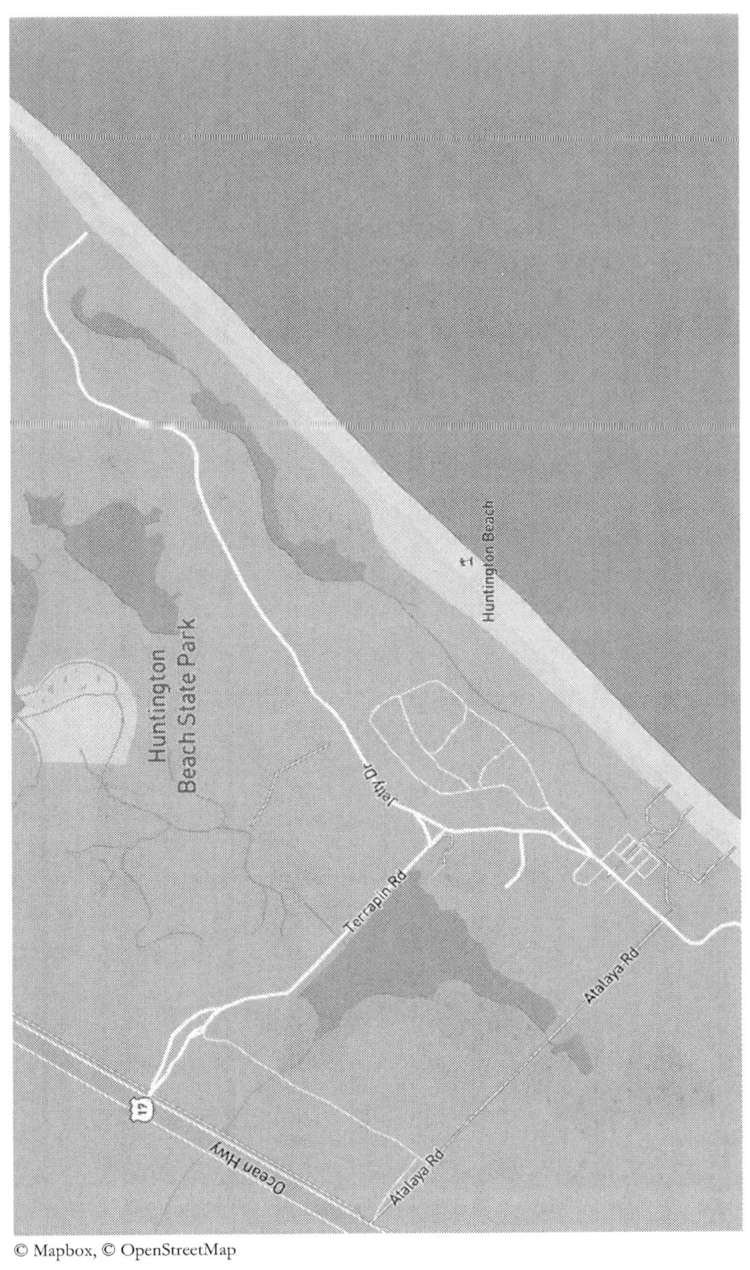

© Mapbox, © OpenStreetMap

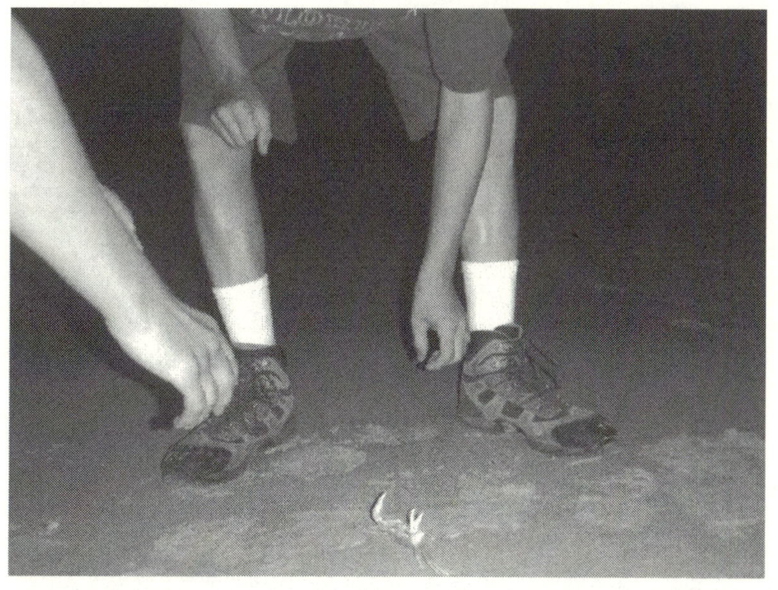

NEW CHINA
120 ITEM BUFFET

Day XXVII

Celebration

Huntington Beach State Park is delightful. We spent our morning swimming and searching for different sea creatures. We found hermit crabs, whelk egg casings, a sea spider, and many more things we'll have to identify. A lot of time was spent in the water body surfing. The waves were perfect for it. The tide was out allowing us to walk out to a sandbar fifty feet out where the water went up only to our knees. There we jumped over the waves as they came. All of us were grinning ear to ear, trying to out-jump the waves and each other.

Near 11:30 a.m. we got out of the water and changed into our nice clothes. Before we went to New China in Surfside Beach, South Carolina, we had to switch trailers with Chief Jeremy and Chief Brian. They drove down to make sure we had the equipment to make it home safely. Running a little late to the restaurant didn't bother us. We were thankful these two were willing to drive down to help. Chief John, our recruiter/trainer and former chief, and Chief Matt, a chief in training, met us at the buffet. They spent the weekend in Myrtle Beach and drove forty-five minutes south to meet us.

We took a picture in front of the restaurant before we went in. Four weeks of waiting was only minutes away now. A chief and a few boys sat at a table for four. We were all close enough to hear and talk between tables. We scoured the buffet looking for what we had dreamt about on the river. I ate a lot but didn't make myself too uncomfortable like I'd done on other celebration meals. The boys weren't as wise when it came to knowing their gastronomical limits. A lot of them needed to go to the bathroom before the meal was finished. They smiled in pain as they recognized their gluttony a little too late. After we could eat no more, Chief John took another group picture of us outside on the way to the van.

Back at the park, one of the park's employees walked through our area verifying campsites. He got me off to the side and said we had to move. Surprised, I showed him our papers saying we could be here. He replied that this was the site for tent camping, not primitive camping. Enlightened of our error, I pleaded for us to stay where we were. I didn't want a move to halt our celebration. It's crazy how quick attitudes can turn, and I did not want this news to upset the boys. Unfortunately, our site was already reserved, and the tenants for the night were supposed to arrive within a few hours. This new area was supposed to be a lot more open and secluded, but it meant we had to move everything back onto the trailer.

We packed everything onto the bus and trailer and moved to the primitive campsite. It was a little troublesome, but we got it taken care of without much complaining. Chief Mike, Chief Travis, and my attitudes set the tone for the group. We didn't act annoyed by the situation, so the boys didn't consider it an annoyance either, they just knew it was something we had to do.

When we set up camp again, we cleaned tents and left them set up to dry, anticipating a good night to sleep under the stars. For supper, we had a small meal. No one was hungry after the buffet. We worked on academics for half an hour when everything from our meal was put away.

When dusk approached, we discussed a plan for a ghost crab ramble. We walked to the beach when it was dark, and the four chiefs shined our headlights, looking for the small white crabs. At first, we didn't find many, but as we walked around our eyes got accustomed to spotting the crustaceans. Everyone chased after them, and lighthearted arguments transpired over who was going to pick up the crab once it was caught.

At first, some of the more timid boys threw a hat over the crab then slowly lifted the hat to catch them. Progressively, they got used to catching them and used the hat only to corral them. I think everyone held a crab and most caught one, a lot of them with no aid of the hat. One drew blood on my hand when I moved its claws for someone to catch. One benefit of changing locations this afternoon was the privacy we now had. No one was at our part of the beach.

On the way back to campsite, Zach became upset. He wouldn't say what it was at first. Someone gathered the group to talk about it; they were concerned with his mood. He deflected questions with "I'm fine" and walked quickly to avoid those checking in on him. Rather than talk with everyone about it, he asked to talk with me one-on-one.

He said he felt like I didn't want him around. I was shocked, but I let him explain himself. He said I kept trying to shut him up or not talk about what he wanted to talk about. As soon as I heard him say it, I knew he was right. When we were walking back, he was excited and talkative. I kept trying to calm him down so we would be set up for a settled pow-wow. In doing this I totally disregarded his feelings.

I made it clear that even after a week or so, I already deeply cared for him, just for being Zach. I'm thankful he was willing to talk with me about it. I feel terrible that he felt that way. I care and try to show care for him. I need to be doing more relationship building than noting when he is doing something wrong.

I pray it was resolved, and there are no grudges. Being so new, I want to give him more grace and explain myself and how camp works more than I would with someone else. I have to establish a trusting relationship with him rather than assume it exists.

Pow-wow highlighted the milestones of the trip. The question tonight was, "What are you proud of?" The question helped draw out some of the trip's events and situations where the guys took ownership. The discussion revolved around helpfulness, whether it was one of the many Good Samaritans who helped us along the river or a group member helping another.

12:30 a.m.

Group Journal: Day 27

We woke up in a campground getting swimming suits on and airing some things out. After we applied sunscreen we headed out to the beach. When we started to head out a kind Samaritan told us there was a shortcut which had less people. We took that way so we could stay focused on our group.

When we got to the beach we wanted to take our swim test to not have to wear lifejackets. Everyone did well; just a few had to wear lifejackets just to be safe. We got a plan and we jumped in right away. I had Logan and Jaylen as my partners for buddies. We had buddies for swimming just in case we get sucked out. It started out with swimming but then it turned into exploring. We found a lot of cool things. We found some sea cucumbers, crabs, and some other things. We saw a loggerhead sea turtle nest. You could tell that it was done the night before or early this morning. We practiced some long jump stuff and went back to swimming.

Next was my most favorite thing. We ate out at a China buffet called New China. It had one hundred and twenty items in it. The best part of the buffet was the sweet and sour chicken. I also enjoyed some vegetable lo mein. We stuffed ourselves silly. Chief John and Chief Matt came with us. They enjoyed a lot of food too. After we ate, we came back to the campsite we were staying at. We found out we were at the wrong one so we had to move. We moved to a place much bigger than the last one we were at. We ate a packed lunch for dinner so it was more of a snack instead of a meal. We did this because we were still really full from our huge lunch.

After we ate, we did some paperwork. I worked on math. We stopped doing that to go to the beach and ramble for ghost crabs. It was fun watching people catch crabs for the first time. We did that for some long while, and then we went to pow-wow and slept under the stars.

Caleb

Day XXVIII

375 Miles

Our night under the stars went well. After the venue change at Huntington Beach State Park, we, as a group, decided to clean our tents in preparation for the mass cleaning when we returned to camp. Since our tents were being aired out and we did not want to dirty them up again, we slept in a line on top of a tarp. The Milky Way shown faintly as I fell asleep, staring at its beauty. I had to get up several times to use the bathroom. After the boys went to bed, I drank almost all the monstrous Bolthouse Farm juice that Chief Adam brought me. He had gotten all three chiefs their drink of choice. It was something special, a gesture that let us know he cares. Throughout the trip I had dreams of a quality puree drink. I was thankful to receive Bolthouse Farms' Green Goodness.

Breakfast was a quick, cold meal. We cleaned up and loaded everything in the trailer by 9:00 a.m. This was no small feat. Everyone used good teamwork, and we were able to maximize our time. The beach was our next stop since we did so well packing our gear. We body surfed the three-foot waves until 10:45 a.m. I felt a sense of relaxation and peace out there playing in the water. The joy of completing one of the biggest trips in Cameron Boys Camp history ran through our veins. Everyone rode, jumped over, or dove under the waves grinning ear to ear.

The ride home was productive with academics and recapping memories of the river with the person sharing their seat. By retelling stories, we begin to solidify them as stories we will remember forever. The more everyone talks about our stories of growth, the more the boys will be inspired by their amazing accomplishments. We got back to camp and unloaded quickly. Almost everything is done and put away. Again, this is a testament to how efficient a well-functioning group can work. Finishing up should only take part of the morning tomorrow.

The Ocmulgee/Oconee/Altamaha Trip was the best trip I've been on. We grew exponentially, due to our hard work. Two twenty-five mile days back to back set us up to meet Chris Bass. Jaylen overcame his nervousness and asked Gregg Boone for a tour of his shrimp boat. Tyler and I devised a plan to catch a baby alligator, an event that will be ingrained in our memories forever.

Playing hard also helped us grow. All the laughing we did while playing Canoe Ball or Stealth melted away the stress we had at the beginning of the trip. I still can't believe Mitchell intentionally tumped our canoe.

Will became more caring for his group and his family. Zach is starting off on the right foot and is also communicating when he doesn't feel right about something. Robert asked good questions and motivated others to work hard. Logan has become more comfortable with himself and doing what's right not because it's cool but because it's right.

Educationally, we grew much faster than we could have in a classroom. Chad flipped through so many pages of our Audubons to figure out the names of the creatures we saw. Caleb realized the importance of selflessness and began to practice that trait more diligently on the last part of the trip.

Everyone struggled through problems. We aren't the same people we were when we started this journey. Noticeable and permanent changes were made on these three rivers. I'm proud of the progress we've made. We can chalk up our three hundred and seventy-five mile trip as a success on all accounts. I am eternally grateful to have this experience with my boys.

10:38 p.m.

Group Journal: Day 28

My journal entry.

"The function of education… is to teach one to think intensively and to think critically… Intelligence plus character – that is the goal of true education."

Dr. Martin Luther King Jr.[9]

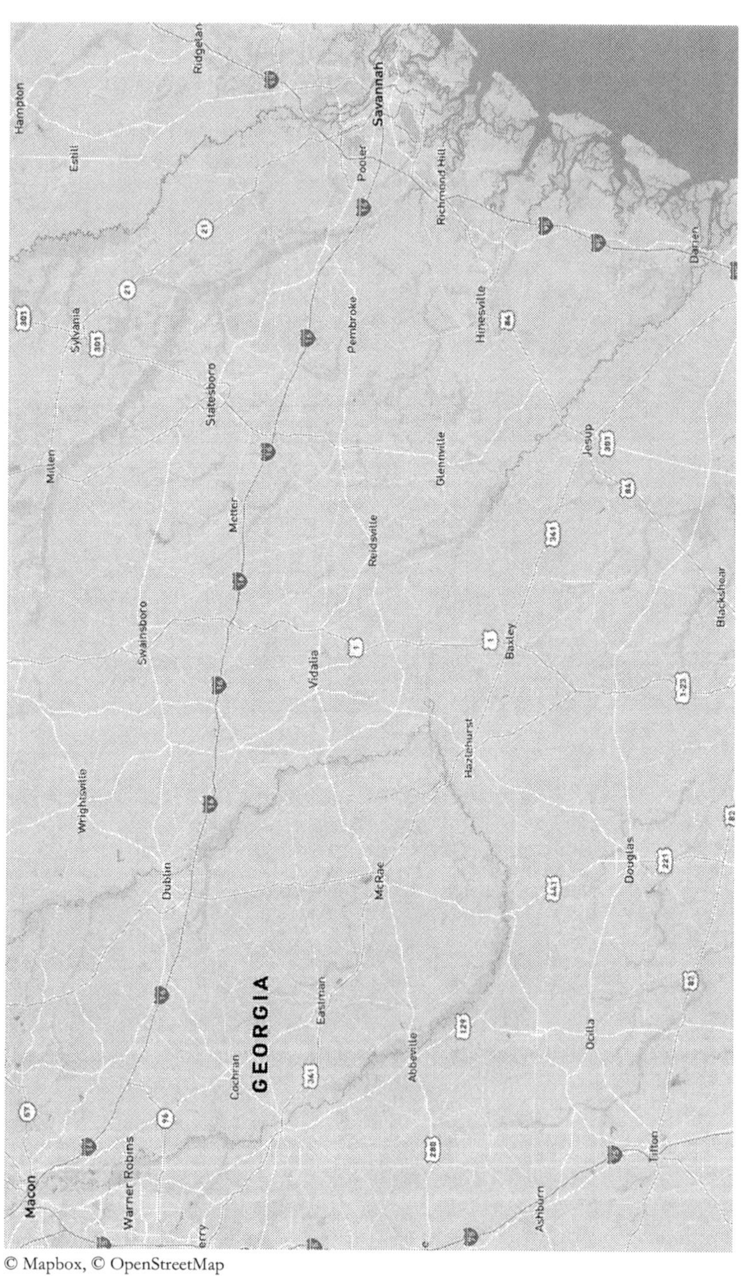
Hampton
Ridgeland
Estill
Savannah
Pooler
Richmond Hill
Sylvania
Hinesville
Pembroke
Darien
Statesboro
Millen
Glennville
Jesup
Metter
Reidsville
Swainsboro
Vidalia
Baxley
Blackshear
Hazlehurst
Wrightsville
Dublin
McRae
Douglas
GEORGIA
Eastman
Cochran
Abbeville
Ocilla
Macon
Warner Robins
Tifton
Ashburn

Epilogue

We left struggles on the river and came back with newfound confidence, looking headstrong at issues that would have caused us to crumble before. The boys also came back with an experience few other high schools have.

Adventure empowered these boys to do hard things. They succeeded because they wanted to help themselves and help others. They stuck together and never gave up. They learned to communicate their feelings more appropriately and to listen, to truly listen, to what other people are feeling. They weren't the only ones to grow. I grew and so did my co-chiefs. I'm a better person because we chose to undertake this endeavor together.

After the trip, the group continued their Cameron Boys Camp experience. They built tents, took other trips, and one by one, returned home to be with their families. As much as I love them I want every boy to leave. They're supposed to be with their families. New guys transitioned in. Those guys didn't make the group worse or better, just different. Camp kept moving forward.

It's been several years since the trip. I haven't had much contact with the boys since they left, but recently I've been able to catch up with a few. The following is a brief description of what I know of their lives now.

Logan

Camp taught Logan how to prioritize needs before wants and also gave him the skills to work as a team. Logan moved to Kansas City with his newly wed wife and child. He started a landscaping company while in KC, sold it, and recently moved back to North Carolina as a family of five.

Will

After camp, Will lived at home briefly, then spent time in prison. He is out, lives in North Carolina, and has a stable job. When he's not at work, he volunteers at a homeless community center. Camping and reading are still enjoyable pastimes. While he acknowledged there's always room for him to grow, he understands the effort and vulnerability it takes to make relationships work.

Robert

Robert went back home earlier than I would have liked, but he's still retained skills to help him succeed. Camp taught Robert to trust others, and find healthy outlets for his anger. Robert has been servicing and repairing big rigs for three years. He is engaged with plans to be married in the fall of 2020.

He has a three-year-old son from a previous relationship. With primary custody, he wants to be a good father. Robert plans to adopt his fiancé's daughter, because he sees the importace of a child having a father.

Mitchell

I haven't been able to reach Mitchell. He left camp just before his eighteenth birthday. He worked through so much while at camp, but there were several things he didn't want to let go of. He has the skills to succeed. I hope he's used them.

Chad

Chad returned home to his mom and little brother. While Chad was in the process of repairing his relationship with his dad, his dad passed away suddenly. He took his father's passing extraordinarily hard, but had moved through the grieving process well.

Chad lives on his own, and works at a tire manufacturing plant. He learned responsibility at camp, something he said he applies every day. The plant will be automating several positions in the future. Chad has already made plans to move into a position with no risk of automation.

Caleb

Caleb moved back to his home state of Pennsylvania. He lived independently for a while, but made the decision to move back home to provide for his mom and younger siblings. Although he wanted to live his own life, he coulndn't watch his family drown. He believes he found the balance of contributing to the family and not taking control. Two months ago, Caleb moved with his family to North Dakota and is working full time cutting electrical wire for vehicle harnesses.

Zach

Zach did not leave camp on a good note. It broke my heart, but it was a choice he wanted to make. Thankfully, he participated in another program (which I was able to be his mentor) and he graduated successfully. The last time I spoke with him was over two years ago. Three weeks ago I heard back from him. He said he's had crazy ups and downs and would like to catch up, but contact has been inconsistent.

Tyler

Tyler misses all the adventures he had at camp. He left camp and lived with his dad. Tyler's love for snakes hasn't faded. He'll often go out of his way to interact with them. We've connected sporadically after he left. One of the last conversations we had was about how much camp has impacted both our lives. He works for a tree and logging company with the goal of managing a crew soon.

Jaylen

Despite multiple tries, I haven't been able to get up with Jaylen. As far as I know when he left camp he went back to school and was doing well.

Chief Mike

Chief Mike left camp shortly after the trip. He moved to Seoul, South Korea as an English teacher for two years, then returned to the United States about the time Hurricane Sandy hit the Northeast coast. He worked with a relief organization in New York City, then returned to North Carolina to marry a supervisor from Camp Duncan. He became a high school teacher and volunteered with Young Life. He and his wife are currently on sabitical, traveling and spending time with family.

Chief Travis

Travis moved to the youngest group, the Frontiersmen, to finish his two-year commitment. He left camp to get married, and move to his old stomping ground in Pennsylvania. In March, Travis and his wife welcomed their first child.

Chief Jason

I spent six more months in the group then transitioned to groupwork supervisor. Now, I oversee camp education at Cameron Boys Camp and Camp Duncan for Girls. I didn't anticipate being at camp longer than two years, but God hasn't called me away. Camp has helped me grow more than I ever imagined.

Six months ago, I married Claire, the love of my life. She's everything I wanted and needed in a spouse. I'm thankful I'm hers. She works at Prancing Horse, a therapeutic riding center half an hour away from the camp. We're both blessed to do what we love.

During our days off together, we enjoy hiking, spoiling our collie puppy, Selah, and exploring new places. Claire's my God-given, life-long travel partner. We are enjoying the adventure Jesus Christ, our one and only savior, is leading us on.

References

1. Adler, M. J. (1982). *The paideia proposal: An educational manifesto.* New York, NY: Touchstone Books. p. 50.

2. Tomlin, C. (1995). Brother Friend. On *Inside Your Love* [CD] Independent Record.

3. The story of Zacchaeus: Luke 19:1-10

4. Parable of the two mites: Mark 12:41-44; Luke 21:1-4

5. Sermon on the Mount: Matthew 5-7

6. Daniel's vision: Daniel 10:1-14

7. Morrison, C. A. (2003). *Running the River: Poleboats, Steamboats &Timber Rafts on the Altamaha, Ocmulgee, Oconee & Ohoopee.*. St. Simons Island, GA. Saltmarsh Press.

8. Adaptation from Loren Eiseley's *The Star Thrower.*

9. King Jr., M .L. *The Purpose of Education.* Maroon Tiger. *Jan-Feb 1947.*

Index